A VIEW FROM THE RIM

Also by Phil Pepe

A VIEW FROM
THE RIM: ○

WILLIS REED
ON BASKETBALL

by WILLIS REED
with PHIL PEPE

An Associated Features Book

ILLUSTRATED WITH PHOTOGRAPHS

J. B. Lippincott Company
Philadelphia & New York

TO MY SON KARL VANCE

May this book be an
inspiration to his life

Contents

List of Illustrations

A VIEW FROM THE RIM   ◯

(Darryl Norenberg).

Introduction

The huge crowd was on its feet, its cheers and applause reverberating throughout the big arena, the sound cascading down upon the tall, solitary figure standing in the center of the court—the one wearing number 19 on his blue basketball shirt.

Number 19 shifted his feet nervously, looking somewhat embarrassed as the public address announcer told the crowd of 11,092 and the millions looking in on national television that the layup Willis Reed had just scored gave him a career total of 10,500 points, making him the highest scorer in New York Knickerbocker history.

To give this historic occasion a sense of time and place, Willis Reed's 10,500th point came on Sunday afternoon, January 24, 1971. It came with four minutes and twenty-seven seconds remaining in the second period of a game between the New York Knickerbockers and the Detroit Pistons. It came in the seventh year of the professional basketball career of Willis Reed.

Carl Braun, who had held the record, scored his 10,499 points in twelve seasons with the Knickerbockers.

"Hmmm," said Reed, "that means I've got a few years to go before I'm close to his longevity record."

Before he finishes his career, Willis Reed will no doubt own every New York Knickerbocker record. And yet, great as it is, his record of points scored, rebounds and years of service will not tell the full story of Willis Reed. Part of the story was told on Sunday afternoon, January 24, 1971, when 11,092 people gave him a standing ovation.

If this had been in New York's Madison Square Garden, such an ovation would not have been surprising. But this was in Detroit's Cobo Arena, on foreign terrain, where Willis Reed is usually the loathsome enemy.

That is the true measure of Willis Reed. That is what this man—born in a Louisiana town so small it does not appear on the map—has become.

I was proud. That was the feeling I had standing there in the middle of Cobo Arena. I felt proud . . . and a little embarrassed in front of all those people.

The record didn't come as a complete surprise. The newspapers had been mentioning for weeks that I was on the verge of becoming the all-time scoring leader in the history of the New York Knickerbockers. It was only a matter of when and where it would happen.

Naturally, I was hoping it would be in New York because I wanted to break that record in front of all our fans who have been so wonderful to me. But the way it turned out, with the standing ovation and all, I'm kind of glad it happened on the road.

After the game the reporters asked me if I could remember the first point I ever scored as a Knickerbocker. I couldn't. I still can't. I know it was in 1964 and it was against the Los Angeles Lakers in Madison Square Garden. There was a big crowd there, more people than I had ever seen before at one time. I can also remember I was nervous and scared, playing in my first game in the National Basketball Association (NBA). I was matched up against Gene Wiley and I know I scored 14 points, but I can't remember the first one. I also remember we lost the game.

What's so strange is that even though I cannot remember the first point I scored in pro basketball, I can remember practically every point I ever scored in high school. I guess that's because I attach a special importance to my high school career. After all, it was there that I learned the fundamentals and began developing the basic skills that would help me become a professional.

Standing there in Cobo Arena with 10,500 points to my credit wasn't just an accident. It wasn't something that happened overnight. It was something that I actually began working for the first time I picked up a basketball.

Every time I went out on a basketball court, every shot I took, every time I bounced a basketball, I was working for this day. The teaching I had, the guidance, the conditioning, the hours I practiced—all these things contributed to getting me here.

Success does not come easily and it doesn't come without hard work and practice. You don't become a great basketball player merely by putting on a pair of sneakers. There's a lot more to it.

Not everybody who plays basketball is going to become a great player. Not everybody is going to become a professional. Not everybody is going even to make his high school or college team. But basketball is a game that is great exercise. It's a game you can have a lot of fun playing, not only when you're young, but when you get older.

I know a lot of businessmen who keep in shape by going to a local gym to play basketball with the boys once, twice, even three times a week. Others like to get out in the backyard and shoot baskets with their sons.

Not only is basketball a game you can enjoy years after you have graduated from college, it's also a game that does not require a lot of expensive equipment or a lot of people to play. You can play one-on-one with another player or you can play two men on a side. All you need is a basketball and a hoop, and there are plenty of hoops around. In the city, you'll find one in every schoolyard or playground. In the suburbs, you'll find one in almost every driveway.

When I started playing basketball, I played because I enjoyed it. I still enjoy it. It also happens to be my profession. It's how I earn my living. Instead of going to an office every morning, I go to an arena almost every night, and I take it seriously just as any man takes his job seriously. The Knicks pay me well to play basketball. I'd be a fool not to take it seriously.

So, this is a book about basketball—about basketball as I play it, basketball as the Knicks play it, basketball as the great stars of the NBA play it.

This book will not make you a great basketball player. But maybe it will help you improve your game a little. Or perhaps it will help give you a better understanding and a greater appreciation of the professional game. Or maybe it will help you learn a little more about my New York Knick teammates.

If it does any of these things, then this book will have achieved its objective.

WILLIS REED

New York

(Danny Farrell)

Here I am in the ninth grade when I was 6-5 and clumsy. *(Willis Reed)*

1
Something to Prove

Willis Reed likes to say he was born in "Nowhere, Louisiana." Actually, "Nowhere" is a little town called Hico, which, Reed says, is so small "they don't even have a population." He was born on June 25, 1942, the only child of Willis and Inell Reed. Five days after the birth of his son, Willis Reed, Sr., went into the Army and Willis, Jr., and his mother went to live with his grandparents.

When he was six, his parents moved 10 miles to Bernice, where Willis grew up. Compared to Hico, Bernice was practically a metropolis. "It is two red lights long," Reed says. "Hico has no red lights, just a couple of stop signs."

Mine was a happy childhood. As an only child, I always had everything I needed. I wasn't deprived, but I wasn't living a life of luxury either. There was always enough food to eat and clothes to wear, although I was growing so fast, it seemed my clothes never fitted me for more than a few months. Most kids in town wore their clothes until they were worn out. Not me. I never had clothes that fitted me long enough for them to wear out.

My mother and father both worked very hard. Dad drove a truck. He loves life, and it's from him that I get my love for the outdoors, fishing and hunting. It's also from Dad that I inherited my height. He stands 6 feet, 4 inches.

Mom is much shorter—about 5–4 and on the plump side. But I always think of her as a woman with great strength and courage. She worked as a domestic, and both my parents instilled in me, from the time I was little, that if you want something, you must work for it. Their attitude was that they worked hard for what they had and so I must work too.

"If you want something," Dad often said, "go out and earn the money to buy it."

It was a good lesson, one I never forgot. I never felt that because I was an only child I was going to get whatever I wanted just by asking for it. I had to go out and do things for myself.

For as long as I can remember, I always had a job. When I was little, I worked in flower beds and picked cotton. The going rate for cotton was three dollars for a hundred pounds. When I got older, I did heavier work, such as hauling hay.

I never regretted working. I enjoyed it. It was the only way I could make money to buy things, like a bicycle and a basketball and hoop. I cut grass and saved up enough money to buy a lawn mower to increase my business.

When I got older, I used the money I earned to buy my own clothes. The heavy work I did helped me develop my body. So there really was no reason for me to regret how hard I worked as a boy. The thing was, I didn't have to work; I wanted to so that I could buy the things I wanted. It gave me a feeling of independence.

As a boy, I always loved sports. We played them all— baseball, basketball and football, depending on what season it was. When the baseball season ended, everybody put away his baseball and took out his football, and when football ended, we put away our football and got out our basketball. Basketball was nothing special over baseball or football for me in those days. In fact, if I had a favorite, it was football.

I liked the contact. I started playing football when I was in the first grade, but my parents were kind of nervous about it. Like most parents, they were afraid I'd get hurt.

Youngsters are always asking me if it's all right to play more than one sport. As a rule, I recommend staying with one sport, especially after a boy has reached high school. You'll find that you use a different set of muscles in football from the ones you use in basketball. As a result, your muscles are not fully developed and the chance of injury is increased.

There are exceptions to the rules, however. If a boy is particularly strong or especially good in more than one sport, it's all right for him to play more than one while he is trying to decide which one he will concentrate on. I think he should experiment with all sports until he finds the one for which he is best suited.

I don't think football will hurt a boy. In fact, I think it makes him a better man to go out and get hit a few times. Playing football in high school was good for me because I got to be a big man and reached the point where I wasn't afraid of contact, which helped me in basketball. Anybody who doesn't think basketball is a physical game has never spent any time under the basket in the National Basketball Association.

Once a boy decides he is a basketball player, he should be a basketball player and nothing else. He should play as much basketball as he can and also spend as much time as he can watching players who are doing things correctly.

I became a basketball player when I was in the ninth grade, and it happened quite by accident. I wish now that I had started when I was eight or nine, but as I said, football was my game. Actually, I didn't find basketball. It found me.

I became interested in the game during physical education class when I was in the eighth grade. I was 6 feet, 2 inches tall, the biggest kid in the class. I wasn't good, but I was big. So I found myself playing a lot of basketball.

An accident on the first day of summer vacation after I graduated from the eighth grade probably changed my life. I fell off my bicycle and broke my arm and had to wear a cast almost the entire summer. I couldn't do a thing that whole time—I just sat around the house, eating and growing.

By the time I entered the ninth grade, I had grown 3 inches, but my mother refused to allow me to play football because of my broken arm. One day, Lendon Stone, the basketball coach, saw me and asked me how tall I was. When I said I wasn't sure, he took me down and measured me. I was 6–5, so he put me on the basketball team.

I had no concept of basketball at all, and whatever coordination I might have had as an eighth grader was gone because of the 3 inches I had grown during the summer. I could be walking down the street and I'd stumble over my own feet I was so clumsy. But I became a basketball player, and because I was so big and only thirteen years old, Coach Stone worked with me—on basic stuff like how to hold the ball, how to shoot the jump shot, how to dribble. I mean I was really starting from scratch.

The first game I ever played in high school, I scored 4 points. In the next game I scored 2 points, and that really bothered me because I was 2 points below my average. We lost both games. In our next game, we went to Haynesville and won our first game in overtime. I scored 23 points. That was the highlight of my life up to then.

Now I was really hooked on basketball. I still wasn't very well coordinated and I had very little experience in the game. Most of the kids I was playing against were more experienced and more skilled than I was and that made me want to improve. I was the biggest kid in the school, and when you're big people expect you to be good and if you're not, it's embarrassing. I had one more problem to overcome. I had never played in front of a crowd and now I was beginning to play with people watching. I had to get over my shyness.

I began to do a little figuring. Since I was so big, it looked like basketball was going to be my game; as long as basketball was going to be my game, I figured I'd better start improving. Once I became interested in basketball, I spent a lot of time on it. I would practice in school, then go home and practice some more on my own. It was cold out and I'd have to practice with a jacket on. Sometimes it would get so cold, I'd go inside and warm my hands, then run back out and play some more.

We played on a dirt court and I'd go home all dirty. We'd never stop playing if it started to rain and then I'd go home with my shoes all covered with mud. I practiced every day. If we had enough players, we'd scrimmage. If not, I practiced by myself.

I'm a great believer in practice. I believe that's the only way to improve your skills. But there's a good side to practice and a bad side. If it's constructive practice, that's fine. But there are youngsters who will go out and practice five or six hours a day on shooting and it will not mean a thing if they're doing everything all wrong, if they're not giving complete concentration to what they're doing. They might just as well not have taken the trouble.

I have a favorite slogan which I had printed on cards and put up on the walls of the gym at my summer basketball camp in Cornwall, New York. The slogan is: BE A CHAMPION IN PRACTICE. THAT'S WHERE CHAMPIONS ARE MADE.

You can achieve more with an hour of good practice, concentrating and doing the right thing, than you can with three or four hours of bad practice, not concentrating, doing things wrong and forming bad habits that will be difficult to break.

Having the proper supervision is very important. If the supervision is not right, the practice session will be almost worthless. I think three hours of basketball can get to be boring. A short practice—but a good one—is so much more beneficial. Once you learn how to do things right, then you can go out on your own and work on that skill.

When I was growing up, I liked to practice a lot on my own to perfect my shot. Then I would scrimmage and experiment with the shot to see if I was doing it right.

When I was a kid, I never had anybody to teach me the right way of doing things. The first teacher I ever had was my high school coach, Lendon Stone. He not only taught

In case you're not sure, I'm number 8, next to my coach, Lendon Stone.
(Willis Reed)

me, he inspired me, encouraged me and increased my love and my interest for the game. He gave me the encouragement I needed to practice and develop my skills.

The one thing I could always do was shoot. Coach Stone said I had a natural, soft shooting touch. Touch is something that cannot be acquired, you either have it or you don't. You can't teach a boy to be a great shooter; all you can do is give him the proper instruction to help him improve the shooting skills he already has. Then the improvement is up to him and how much he practices. But, basically, a shooting touch is a natural thing.

I was uncoordinated, didn't know how to move, and knew practically nothing about the fundamentals of the game, but my basketball career was launched in my freshman year in high school because of two things I had absolutely nothing to do with—my height and a natural, soft shooting touch, both God-given.

I could feel myself developing in my freshman year. I had a lot of up-and-down games, but it was just a matter of becoming sure of the few skills I had and trying to develop new ones. I practiced learning to pivot left and right, learning how to dribble with either hand, going in for layups. These were the basic, fundamental skills of the game that would stay with me for as long as I played, and I was trying to refine them, to get them to become almost automatic. It wasn't easy. These were new skills for me and they were unnatural. I felt awkward doing them. The hardest thing for me to develop was to fake one way and turn the other—head fakes, shoulder fakes, any kind of fake. By then my body still had not developed to the point where I could fake easily and comfortably.

I could feel improvement with each game. I averaged about 12 points a game for my freshman year, which I didn't think was too bad. But I still had a long way to go.

In addition to improving my skills, I was gaining confidence. I knew my sophomore year was going to be a good one and it was. I grew another inch to 6–6 and averaged 17.5 points a game, but more important as far as the development of my character was concerned was an incident in a game during that season. I got what I thought was a bad call from an official and I expressed my dissatisfaction with the call in an immature, outspoken manner.

It was the wrong thing to do and Coach Stone let me know it. He jumped off the bench and yanked me out of the game. Among other things, he pointed out that the official could slap me with a technical foul, which would hurt my team.

"You're finished for the night," Coach Stone said. "Go in and take that uniform off. You'll keep it off until you prove to me that you're man enough to wear the school colors and to represent the school in the manner you should represent it."

I didn't think so at the time, but I realize now that Coach Stone was right and I'll never forget him for teaching me that lesson. I acted like a child. There is no room in a team sport for a prima donna. No player is more important than the team, which is the principle that made the New York Knickerbockers champions of the world.

My interest in basketball was such that I began to become aware of the pros and to try to do things the way they did them. I started watching the *NBA Game of the Week* on television, and the player I most admired was Bill Russell. I admired him not only for his great ability but for other reasons as well. It seemed we had a lot in common. I started playing ball in 1956 and that was the year Russell joined the Celtics; he was a center and I was a center; he was left-handed and I was left-handed; he was born in Louisiana and I was born in Louisiana. So he kind of became my man. I remember that when I was in high school and I would block a shot on somebody, I would think to myself that this was the way Russell did it. That always stuck with me. I always wanted to be a good center and rebounder like Russell was.

Another man I admired was Bob Pettit, also a Louisiana boy. We used to pick up radio station WMOX from St. Louis, and I listened to the Hawks' games and became a Hawks fan. I admired Pettit for his fortitude and determination. Here was a man who came to play every night, a man who got the job done and had the courage to play when he was hurt. Once he played with a cast on his shooting hand. I remember reading a story about him, and the thing that impressed me was that he was unable to make his high school team. It surprised me because he was one of the superstars of pro basketball, and I knew the only way he got there was by hard work and determination. It not only told me something about him; it also told me something about what you can accomplish if you work hard.

I wouldn't say that the thought of playing professional basketball was always on my mind when I was in high school. I thought about it, but I didn't dwell on it. It was more like a dream. You know, it might be a gloomy day or a hot, lazy one and I'd be sitting under a shade tree, letting my mind wander. I'd kind of lose myself, thinking about the big time. I'd imagine myself one day playing against all those great pros and having all that fame. It seemed just like that—a dream. It seemed such a remote thing in those days, something you dream about which never comes true. It wasn't until I was in college that I got the feeling that my dream was not that remote after all.

From the way we finished in my sophomore year in high school, I knew we were going to be tough to beat the following year. I averaged 25 points a game as a junior and I began to get my name in the local papers regularly. I also began to get a bit of a rush from college scouts. I was feeling pretty good until late in the year when we lost the state championship. I should say *I* lost the state championship—but I learned a valuable lesson.

In the championship game I was called for traveling about five or six times, which probably was the difference between winning and losing. You'll remember that earlier I talked about picking up bad habits that are hard to break. That was what happened to me. All season long I had used a move out of the pivot that I picked up in a coaching magazine.

The way it worked was that with my back to the basket, I would step to the right on a feint, leaning to my right on my right foot, thereby establishing my left foot as my pivot foot. Then, stretched out to my right, I would move my left foot slightly to spin around and shoot my jumper. That's how I thought the play was diagrammed. But I was traveling and, as I said, I got away with it all season, so I never realized I was traveling. But in the state championships the officiating was better and the officials picked it right up and called it and we lost the game.

We made up for it in my senior year, winning the state championship. By then I had grown to my present height. While I'm on the subject of height, let me clear up one thing right here and now.

My height has been listed as anywhere from 6–8 to 6–11. I've even read that I'm probably shorter than 6–8. Well, this is the truth—I'm 6–10. Actually, I'm not quite 6–10, but I'm not 6–9 either. I'm somewhere between 6–9 and 6–10, but I'm closer to 6–10 than I am to 6–9. I was always taught that when something is more than half, you go to the next whole number. So I consider myself 6–10.

Anyway, I had grown to my full height of 6–10 by my senior year in high school. We had a tough team, a team just like the Knicks: guys who really played together, pulled together, did everything together. We won the state championship and I averaged 28 points a game. I had dozens of college offers. You couldn't ask for more. It was almost a perfect year.

I say it was "almost" a perfect year because one thing continued to bother me. I figured I was a pretty good basketball player and people told me I was good, but how good was I? I really didn't know. I don't think a player ever really knows how good he is.

For instance, was I doing things on the same caliber as a kid playing center in, say, California, Ohio, Indiana, New York or some of those other places where good basketball is played? I had no criterion by which to judge myself.

I didn't even know if I was the best center in the State of Louisiana. Many schools there were better than mine because they were bigger. In Louisiana, you play in your own classification, which is determined by the number of students in the school. My school, Westside Consolidated, was in the AA classification because we had only a hundred boys. In a large school, would I have been able to make the team as the starting center? I didn't know, and not knowing bothered me. I wanted to find out how good I was.

For all my success in high school, winning the state championship and making the All-State team and everything, I still didn't feel as if I had done anything special. I never got the attitude that I was that great. All through high school, I always felt I still had something to prove.

I didn't set the world on fire as a Grambling freshman. *(Westside High School)*

2
I Never Want to Find Out

In May of his sophomore year in high school, Willis Reed and a friend took a trip to the town of Ruston. Ruston is the "big city" in northwest Louisiana, 21 miles from Bernice, 5 miles from the campus of Grambling College.

Waiting at the bus stop for the return trip to Bernice, Reed was approached by a tall, cigar-smoking stranger.

"What's your name, son?" the stranger asked.

"Willis Reed."

"How tall are you?"

"Six-six."

The stranger continued asking questions: what high school did Reed attend, what year was he in, how old was he, what sports did he play, what were his grades?

"It was all very casual," Reed remembers.

Then the stranger said: "Son, my name is Fred Hobdy. I'm the basketball coach at Grambling. I want to tell you, when you finish school at Westside, you come on down to Grambling and look me up and I'll give you a scholarship."

When Coach Hobdy told me that, I was so excited I could hardly wait to get home to tell my mother. Naturally she was happy, and it made me feel good to see her so pleased. I guess I decided, then and there, that I would attend Grambling College, although I had offers to go to bigger schools when I graduated from high school.

One of the main reasons I wanted to go to Grambling was that it was close to home and my folks would be able to see me play ball in college. I guess Mom helped influence me too. Since I was an only child, she didn't want me to go too far away from home. I realized some years later that she had a lot to do with my decision. One day I heard Coach Hobdy talking about recruiting.

"Get the mother," he said, "and you get the son."

I guess he worked on Mom pretty good.

One of the things Coach Hobdy asked me at the bus station was what sports I played. I said football and basketball.

"Football," he said. "You don't need that. You can get hurt playing football."

Lendon Stone, my high school coach, had gone to Southern University and he mentioned that he would like me to go there too. But he made it clear that this was a decision I would have to make by myself.

"Wherever you go," he said, "you're going to have to stay four years and you have to be happy. If you go to Southern and you're not happy, I'd be the one to blame."

I appreciate what Coach Stone did and what he said. I was young and I could easily have been influenced to go where he wanted me to go. That's how much I thought of him. But he never pushed me. There are a lot of coaches who try to influence kids on where to go to college and I don't think it's right. It's the boy who has to go to the college and spend four years, and he should make that decision himself, with the help of his parents.

In the end, I went to Grambling. I was sorry to have to disappoint my coach, but I have never had any regrets about going to Grambling. For one thing, Grambling was instrumental in preparing me for the pros because Coach Hobdy played a pro-style game—a lot of running, jumping and shooting, and this is what professional basketball is all about. I couldn't have gone to any other school and expected things to turn out better for me than they did. So, even though Grambling is a small school, I'd have to say going there didn't hurt me one bit as far as my professional career is concerned. In fact, it probably helped.

Grambling was different from most of the schools that wanted me, many of them what you would call basketball powers. Some promised that I could walk right in and be a starter. At Grambling, I had no such guarantee. The only thing Coach Hobdy promised was that I would get a chance to play. I told him that was all I wanted.

Grambling had a sophomore center named Tommy Bowens, a player with great potential. He was going to be there for three of my four years and I knew I had to beat him out to get a starting job, but I decided to take the chance.

Freshmen were eligible for varsity ball at Grambling and I made the squad in my first year, but I didn't exactly set the world on fire.

That first summer I did some of the hardest running I ever did in my life. Run, run, run. I began to wonder if I had gone out for basketball or for cross-country. We used to run so much, I dreaded the thought of going to practice. And Coach Hobdy used to get on us pretty good. He'd say we just didn't love the game of basketball enough.

"You guys can't wait to quit," he would say. "You don't like to practice. And if you don't like practice, you don't like basketball. Me, I get itchy. I just can't wait to get over here to practice."

I remember thinking: "Sure, you're itchy. I'd be itchy too if all I had to do was sit up there and watch somebody else run."

Of course, Coach Hobdy knew what he was doing. All that running was for a purpose. It was going to pay off for us eventually. The things we did in practice at Grambling were the first steps toward making me into a basketball player; I mean a basketball player tailored for professional ball.

We used to jump rope and lift weights and go through all kinds of jumping drills. We had to jump up and touch the rim five times first with our right hand, then five times with our left hand and finally five times with both hands, alternating left and right. We'd practice rebounding the ball over the basket, that is, tip it over the basket. Then someone would throw it over the basket and we'd have to go up, catch it, control the ball and shoot it at the basket, or go up, catch it and dunk it.

Coach Hobdy has good success with big boys. He believes in the overload principle, overloading a boy with work. That is, you would work much harder than you had to work to produce, but the level at which you produced was always a little higher than it was for those who didn't work so hard.

One of his favorite drills was the "flying three." Three men would break at top speed from one end of the court and have to score at the other end. If they didn't make the layup, they would have to do it all over again. Sometimes we had only nine men and we'd take turns running the flying three for twenty minutes, up and down, always at top speed. You can't imagine how tired you can get running a flying three for twenty minutes.

When there were fifteen minutes left in the practice, we'd stop and shoot our free throws. Then we'd do our jumping drills and finish up by just running for the last three minutes.

Coach Hobdy, like a lot of coaches, liked to have us shoot our free throws when we were tired. He believed in the old theory that if you can make free throws when you're tired, you certainly should be able to make them when you're fresh. Also, there will be times in a big game when you'll have to step to the free-throw line when you're very tired.

You hear a lot about first-half teams and second-half teams. The Knicks are noted for being a second-half team. That's not just an accident; that's all part of conditioning. A well-conditioned team will be able to do things in the second half when other teams that are not so well-conditioned might be just a little bit tired. If you can get to the point where you can consistently do things when you're tired, you're going to be a much better ballplayer.

One thing stands out in my mind from those practice sessions in my freshman year. We were scrimmaging one night, and I remember shooting a hook shot on the move, going to my right. The defensive man went up to try to block the shot. As he went up with the shot, I moved around him, caught the rebound with one hand and jammed it into the basket.

Coach Hobdy stopped the practice and called me over. "Let me tell you something," he said. "Before you leave Grambling, you're going to be an All-American."

That made me feel good. After I had made All-State in high school, my one ambition was to become a college All-American and have my picture taken with all the great basketball players all around the country.

The first few games in my freshman year, I shared the center position with Tommy Bowens. Then we went to New Orleans to play a game against Dillard University. They had a very tiny gym and they were up for us because they were a little school and we were one of the bigger basketball powers in the area.

I played a little in the first half, enough to score 5 points, and I rebounded well. At half time, Coach Hobdy said: "You look like you want to play ball tonight. I'm going to put you in in the second half and see what you can do."

But I never did get back in and I was disappointed. I was getting to the point where I would go to bed at night and couldn't sleep from thinking about how badly I wanted to make the team.

Just about that time something important happened. It was during Christmas vacation and we were practicing and I was kind of dragging. I had a toothache and didn't feel like practicing, and Coach Hobdy was getting on me pretty good. He didn't believe I was hurting; he thought I was begging off. I went to my room and started packing my stuff. I was going to quit and go home.

Charlie Hardnett, my teammate, came by and said, "Don't let the coach get next to you." But I had made up my mind to go home.

Then Howard Willis came to see me. He had been a center at Grambling before me and he was helping Coach Hobdy with the team while finishing up his studies. He used to work with me on the jumping drills. Howard Willis was a really fine man who was nicknamed "Jim Dandy" because at the time he was playing, there was a popular song with a line in it that went, "Jim Dandy to the rescue."

Jim Dandy really came to my rescue. He told me that when he was in school, he was having some personal problems and he, too, almost quit. Somebody talked him out of it, and he stayed and got his degree. Now he was going to pass that advice on to me.

Coach Willis got me together with Coach Hobdy, and I was able to convince him that I really did have a toothache, that I wasn't jaking. He said, "All right, tomorrow we'll send you to the dentist." I ended up having the tooth extracted, which is a painful way to prove a point.

Coach Willis saved me from making a terrible mistake. He kept me from packing up and going home, and I appreciate it. I always will. Maybe I can pass that favor along to someone else. Maybe I can do it through this book. When things get rough, don't quit. Stick it out. Everybody gets to feeling that he'd like to quit at some time or another, but quitting never proved anything. It takes courage to stick it out when the going is tough, but in the long run you'll find out it's worth it, as I did.

Soon after the first of the year, I finally got my chance to play. We went to Southern University, and as the game was about to start and Tommy was taking off his black and gold warm-up shirt, Coach Hobdy stopped him.

"Hold up," he said. "Reed's starting tonight."

I knew I was going to play a lot that night, but I had no idea I was going to start my first game. I was shocked. I went out and played a good ball game. I grabbed 16 rebounds and scored 19 points. I even tipped in the basket that won the

Against Westminster College in the NAIA tournament in 1961, I had a hot night, making nine of ten from the field on jumpers. *(United Press International Photo)*

game, but the official credited it to Charlie Hardnett. What could I say? I was only a freshman, and he was already an All-American.

From that point on, I started every game. I ended up shooting 61 per cent from the field and we won the NAIA (National Association of Intercollegiate Athletics) championship in my freshman year. I made honorable mention on the NAIA All-American team. I averaged only 12 points a game on a team that averaged almost 100 points a game, but I didn't get to take many shots. By the time guys like Charlie Hardnett, Herschel West, Rex Tippitt and Bobby Ricks got through, there weren't any shots left for me to take. I got the leftovers.

Two of the biggest games I had all year were in the NAIA playoffs. We came up against Westminster College, which had beaten Winston-Salem the year before by playing a slowdown offense. They slowed down against us, too, but we beat them. I made nine of ten from the field and two out of two from the foul line to score 20 of my team's 45 points. The funny thing about that game is that all nine baskets I made were on jumpers from the top of the key. The one I missed was from inside the foul lane—the closest shot I had all night and I missed it.

We beat Georgetown of Kentucky for the championship, and in that final game I scored 21 points. I was beginning to come into my own, to gain confidence and to improve.

The important thing in college, the reason for my improvement, was that now I was playing against big men all the time. In high school, I rarely faced anyone my size; now every team we played had at least one player as tall as me or taller. Even in practice, I played against big guys. It meant I had to consistently put out to do well.

I always felt I could shoot with anyone in our league, but I needed improvement in other parts of my game. Working at them helped me improve. One thing I learned was how to change direction. We had "reaction" drills, and it was something I used to sit down and think about. I would think about how I could maneuver to beat people. You just don't

I'm number 50 this time and I'm making a reverse layup against Fort Hays State in the 1963 NAIA tournament. *(NAIA)*

play this game on instinct alone. Instinct is important, but thinking is important too.

Early in the season you're indecisive and you may be missing shots and making mistakes. But as the season goes on, you begin doing things right. Muscle tone and confidence are building, and all of a sudden you see yourself making moves because you have confidence. The situation comes up, so you make the move. You find yourself reacting much more quickly as the season goes on. The situations keep coming up, you're constantly making moves and before you know it, they have become almost automatic.

By my sophomore year I was beginning to put it all together. I averaged 17 points a game that season and, in my junior year, I was the big man of the team. I averaged 21 points and almost 20 rebounds and I was beginning to get recognition around the country. By recognition I mean the pro scouts were starting to come down to Grambling to look me over because of my size. In professional basketball they are always on the lookout for big men.

My senior year was my best as far as scoring is concerned. I made 50 per cent of my shots from the field and 70 per cent from the foul line and averaged 26.5 points on a team that scored over 90 points a game. I guess I could have scored more, but that wasn't important.

I remember in my senior year in high school, I probably could have scored 35 to 36 points a game, but there were some nights I didn't even have to shoot the ball and we'd win. Many times the coach had to tell me to shoot.

I guess that's something that's just in me—I never worried too much about how many points I scored. I still don't. At my summer basketball camp in upstate New York, one camper asked me if I thought I could be in the top three in scoring in the NBA if I played for a last-place team and got to do most of the shooting. I told him, in all honesty, that I didn't know and I didn't care. I never want to find out. Scoring points is not the objective of basketball. The objective is to win ball games. Isn't it better to score fewer points and win than to score a lot of points and lose? At least that's the way I've always figured it.

Our combined NAIA team finished third among eight in the 1964 U.S. Olympic trials. I'm fourth from the left in the second row, and number 14 is Lucius Jackson. *(NAIA)*

I guess we were all proud—Mom and Dad and me—when my high school
held a Willis Reed Day in 1964. I'm wearing my jacket from the Pan-
American Games. *(Westside High School)*

Anyway, I had a good year as a senior. I scored my points and got my rebounds. We won and that made everything perfect. I could hardly wait until I graduated. I no longer worried about what other centers were doing in other parts of the country as I did when I was a senior in high school.

I could tell by the way the pro scouts started coming around that it wouldn't be long before I was going to get the chance to show what I could do against all those other centers.

As a rookie I had something to prove to myself and to a lot of others.
(*George Kalinsky*)

3
On the Second Round

The telephone rang at Webster High School in Minden, Louisiana, where Willis Reed was student-teaching. The long-distance operator said she had a person-to-person call from New York for a Mr. Willis Reed, Jr. The caller was Eddie Donovan, coach of the New York Knickerbockers.

"Hello, Willis, how are you doing?" Donovan said pleasantly.

"Fine, Mr. Donovan."

"I just wanted you to know that you have been drafted by the New York Knickerbockers . . . on the second round . . ."

There was some more idle chatter, something about the Knicks getting in touch with him and inviting him to New York to discuss terms of his contract, but Willis Reed really didn't hear any of it. He remembers the sudden feeling of exhilaration at hearing he had been drafted by the New York Knicks, then, just as suddenly, the feeling of dejection on hearing he had been drafted on the second round.

It wasn't that I had anything against Eddie Donovan, the Knicks or New York, but I was disappointed. My pride was hurt. I felt certain I was going to be drafted on the first round.

I thought, all along, that I would go to the Detroit Pistons. Earl Lloyd was scouting me, and it seemed that every time Earl saw me play, I had my greatest games. But it just happened that Charlie Wolf, the Pistons' coach, saw Joe Caldwell play a couple of great games and Wolf made up his mind he was going to take Caldwell.

The one time Eddie Donovan came down to see me play, I didn't play well. Actually, I was having a great game, but he arrived late. Just as he walked in, I went for a loose ball, fell awkwardly on my right shoulder and played the rest of the game in pain. He never got a chance to see me play at my best.

The next time he saw me was in the Olympic trials in the spring of 1964 at St. John's University in New York. I was just awful. I had a virus, I couldn't breathe and I got tired just running up and down the court. I didn't feel well enough to play, and the only reason I stayed was that I didn't want to let my college down.

Realistically, I don't think I would have made the Olympic team no matter how well I played. I don't think they were looking at me. I think they had their team pretty well picked even before the trials. Not that I deserved to make it. I didn't. But there were a lot of guys there who did deserve to make it and didn't.

What I'm saying is that I believe the people who picked the team went into the trials with a preconceived idea of which players would make it—the players from the big colleges and with big reputations. Even if those players really fouled up, I still believe they were going to be picked. In a way that's fair to those great players, because you can have a bad two or three games in the trials for any number of reasons and you would miss out on making the Olympics even though you have been a great player throughout your college career. On the other hand, it's not fair to the other players to invite them to participate in the trials although they have no chance in the world of making the team. And that's just what I felt the officials did.

To get back to the pros, I knew the Knicks were looking for a big man and I knew, too, that they had narrowed their search down to three—Jim Barnes of Texas Western, Lucius Jackson of Pan American and me. Jackson and Barnes played in bigger towns where the media were more available; therefore they got more recognition than I did.

In the end the Knicks, who had the first pick, took Barnes. That's not what bothered me. I thought that was a good pick for them. Jim was big, strong, tough and an excellent player when I came up against him in college. He had played well in the trials. I might have picked him, too, if I had to make that decision.

What I couldn't understand is how eight other teams could pass me by. Eight other ball clubs said, "Forget him; he's not worth being a number-one pick." That meant a lot to me, being somebody's number-one draft pick, knowing somebody thought I was the best player in the country, and as I said before, my pride was hurt.

I think the reason I was overlooked was that I played for a black school. I'm saying the reason I was overlooked was not because I am black, but merely because I played for a black school and all-black schools did not then get the attention from the scouts and the press that they get today.

It would be nice to believe that men of professional sports do not concern themselves with the color of a player's skin —not these days anyway. It would be nice to think that their only concern is the good of their ball club, that their only interest is in building a winner. It would be terribly disappointing to know that there are owners in professional basketball who are that narrow in their thinking. I know that's naïve of me, but I think the NBA has the best record in professional sports when it comes to racial justice. If there ever was a quota system, it existed before I came into the league; it certainly does not exist today—or haven't you checked the rosters of NBA teams lately?

You have to remember that I came out of college in 1964, when there were only nine teams in the league. Now there are seventeen teams in the NBA and another professional league, the American Basketball Association. The players have to come from somewhere. Also, scouting has improved so that every school, no matter how small it is, is scouted thoroughly for pro prospects.

There have been so many stars who came out of tiny schools—like Earl Monroe from Winston-Salem, Zelmo Beaty from Prairie View A & M, Bob Dandridge from Norfolk State and Walt Frazier from Southern Illinois—that the pro scouts don't dare overlook any school. They realize you don't have to come from an Ohio State or a Notre Dame or a UCLA to be a great ballplayer.

So, the Knicks drafted me as the first player on the second round after every other team had passed me up, but it all worked out for the best. With everything being equal, New York was the best place for me to be. I was joining a team that was rebuilding, so there was an opportunity to play. And I was going to play in the greatest city in the world, the center of communications and advertising, and that meant that the chance for exposure and outside income was better in New York than anywhere else—if I made good in basketball.

I had never been to New York before and when I first got there, I was a little in awe of the place. I wasn't scared, but I felt insignificant, just a little old country boy in the big city.

I wasn't scared because I had a job to do, I had something to prove, to myself and to a lot of other people. I don't mean the people who passed me on the first round of the draft and I don't mean it made me want to try harder to prove I deserved to be a number-one draft pick. If I had been number one, I would have had to prove that I was deserving of that honor. Either way, there was a challenge.

I've read a lot of stories about how the first day I was in training camp with the Knicks, I asked Mr. Donovan for a rule book. Well, the stories are true. I did ask him for a rule book, but I still don't think that's anything unusual. I knew

My high school idol, Bill Russell, is blocking one of my shots. I hate to think of how many of my shots he blocked. *(United Press International Photo)*

the pros played a different style of ball than the colleges, that some of the rules and interpretations were different. I just wanted to know what those interpretations were, and what better place is there to find out than in the rule book?

If you decide to be a house painter, you start out by making certain you have the best paintbrushes you can get. What I'm saying is, basketball was going to be my life, my profession, so I wanted to be sure I had all the proper tools to do my job to the best of my ability. The rule book was going to help me know which tools I should use.

I won the starting center job and I even made the All-Star team in my rookie year. The thing I remember most about the All-Star game in St. Louis is coming down in the elevator in the Chase Hotel the afternoon of the game. All of a sudden the elevator stopped, the door opened and there I was looking straight at the most famous beard in the NBA.

"Hello, Mr. Reed," Bill Russell said. "Where are you headed?"

I'm just about the same height as Russell, but somehow he appeared to be about 4 or 5 inches taller. I felt like I was looking up at him—or he was looking down at me. He looked so menacing, so diabolical behind that beard. He moved with such grace and with such poise and confidence. Russell has a velvet-smooth voice and an infectious cackle when he laughs, which is often. He has a brilliant mind, so brilliant that sometimes his mind seems to be racing ahead of his voice and he occasionally stammers when he talks. But when he talks, he makes you want to listen to every word.

"I'm going down for my pregame meal," I told Bill Russell.

"Do you mind if I join you?"

Did I mind if he joined me? What a question. Here was my high school idol, the greatest man in the sport at the time, and here I was, a raw rookie, and he was asking to join me for dinner. I had played against him a few times, and we exchanged pleasantries on occasion, but I never really had a chance to have a long conversation with him. There were so many things I wanted to ask him—if I dared.

Bill selected a remote corner table where we weren't likely to be bothered by well-wishers or autograph-seekers. We sat there for more than two hours—a very interesting, very profitable two hours indeed. He did most of the talking and I did most of the listening and what I learned in those two hours was invaluable. What I learned was not technique —how to shoot, how to rebound, how to play defense, that kind of stuff. What I learned was more a philosophy of basketball, Bill Russell's philosophy of basketball.

I wanted to know his theories and he told me; he explained that a lot of mental things went into his game along with his physical attributes. He said he had a mental book on every player in the league, their assets, their liabilities, their habits, their instincts, their moves. He stressed that basketball is not a game you play with your body only; you also play it with your mind. I came away with the idea that you have to learn about the fellows you oppose. You have to know their moves and what you can do against them and what you can't do. You have to be constantly learning the game, to know what that guy's going to do in certain situations and how he's going to do it.

"People are creatures of habit," Bill said. "They're going to react the same way under stress and adversity. I try to learn those actions and instincts and commit them to memory."

Bill shed a whole new light on basketball for me, things I had never thought about. He convinced me that basketball is as much mental as physical, and I vowed to try to employ his philosophy. I vowed to become a mental basketball player as well as a physical one.

I'm still learning. I try to analyze men I play against, to find out what moves I can make. Even during the course of the game, I see if I can get some clue as to what's working and what isn't, what's good and what's bad. Late in the season, I'm still experimenting and I'm still learning, although not as much.

Things change. New players come into the league, and the players already in the league improve, change, adjust, try

something new. So you always have to be improving, changing, adjusting, trying something new yourself. And you always have to be learning.

I can remember very vividly the times I played against
Russell that first year. He was an established star and I was
a rookie, still trying to find out what I could do against him
and what I couldn't do. I learned there was more that I
couldn't do than I could do.

It really wasn't much of a match. He was quicker and I
wasn't confident. He was experienced and I was a rookie. He
played for a championship team and I played for a very poor
team. I wasn't frightened playing against him. Let's just say
I respected him to the utmost.

And I realized there was still an awful lot I had to learn.

Bill Russell taught me some facts of life. *(United Press International Photo)*

As a forward I found myself playing against smaller but quicker opponents. *(George Kalinsky)*

4
Money in the Bank

Rookie of the Year in the NBA, leading scorer for the Knicks and seventh highest in the league with a 19.5 average, named to the All-Star team as a backup center, Willis Reed had made an impressive start in his professional basketball career.

But the Knicks still finished on the bottom of the NBA's Eastern Division in 1964–65. They had improved by nine games over the previous year, but they were still dead last, still nine games away from a playoff spot.

Less than a month had passed in Willis Reed's sophomore season when the Knicks announced a trade. They sent Johnny Green, Johnny Egan and Jim Barnes to Baltimore in exchange for Walt Bellamy.

Bellamy was a veteran of four NBA seasons, an excellent offensive player who had averaged 27 points a game for his four years. Bellamy, who stands 6 feet, 11 inches, was also a center.

When the club traded for Walt Bellamy, I didn't think they were telling me I couldn't play center. I

57

think it was simply that they had a chance to get an experienced big man, something they hadn't had in years, so they made the deal. In a way I should have been flattered because they had confidence in my ability to make the switch from center to forward.

Frankly, I couldn't say the same about my own confidence. I had never played forward. From the first day I began playing basketball back in the ninth grade, I was a center because of my height.

I knew it was going to be tough learning a new position, but I wasn't unhappy about the switch. I recognized that Bellamy was going to be a big asset to our team; I was still a starter and I was still playing in New York. My one regret was that I had to make the change during the season. It would have been better if I had had all of training camp to adjust to my new position, but the club wanted me to play forward so I just had to go out and try to do the job.

The toughest thing was that I was playing against players who were much quicker than the ones I had played against as a center, guys who were much smarter at their position than I was because they had played it so much longer. I mean players like Elgin Baylor, Rick Barry, Jerry Lucas, Ray Scott, Bailey Howell, Chet Walker and Rudy LaRusso.

My biggest problem was on defense. I had to get accustomed to the quickness of these players, and that takes a while. And I had to change my style of defense because you can't give these guys too much room on their outside shot. If you give them an extra step, they'll make their shots. I got into foul trouble because of all these things and fouled out of thirteen games that year.

On offense, you have to learn to play facing the basket all the time and do things like a normal forward does them. Here again, I was grateful for having gone to school at Grambling. In college we played a high post, that is, three men outside, two inside. I was one of the two men inside and we'd alternate. First I would play low (under the basket), while the other man played high (outside near the key). Then we'd switch and I'd go out on the high post. That was our style in college, and when I went on the high post it was almost like playing a forward position.

Then, too, playing as a forward, I was able to take advantage of my shooting ability. One of the reasons I think I developed a good touch on my jumper is that when I was younger, because I was so tall, all the schools used to play a zone defense against us. That meant that all I could do was take the jump shot—just get the ball, turn and shoot. That was the only shot I could get consistently.

I said earlier that you cannot teach a boy a shooting touch, that he is born with it. However, you can help him improve his touch and you can teach him how to shoot a jump shot, the shot that helped revolutionize the game of basketball. Until about fifteen years ago, hardly anybody used the jumper. Now everybody uses it. Probably as much as 75 per cent of the shots from the field in most games are jumpers, and if you don't have a good jump shot, you're going to have a tough time making it.

The first thing you must learn about shooting the jumper is how to hold the ball. Your fingers should be spread, the ball resting on, and controlled by, the fingertips. You mustn't let the ball touch the palm because once you do, you have a tendency to push the ball rather than flip it with the wrist. It's harder to control and puts too much strain on the arm if you push it.

Usually, the first thing you see a youngster do when he picks up a basketball is jam that ball right into the palm of his hand. Then he'll go out too far from the basket and try to shoot. As a result, if his body, or his wrist, is not strong enough, he has a tendency to push the ball or throw it and he will lack accuracy and control. That's another example of bad practice.

The next time you see the Knicks play—or any pro team —pick out your favorite player and watch him when he starts warming up before the game. You'll notice he'll start shooting up close to the basket, until he has the feel of the ball and the range of the basket. Then he'll gradually move farther away.

The correct form on the jumper: eyes on the basket, concentration, wrist locked, middle fingers last to touch the ball, and follow through. *(Farrell)*

The building can be falling down, but Jerry West won't let it break his concentration. *(Wen Roberts, Photography Inc.)*

Your arm should be kept close to your body; your shoulder, elbow and wrist should all be in line and should come straight through, directly parallel to your body, so you don't have forces and angles going off in all different directions. Try to keep the ball in front of you and the hand extended as far as you can. The forearm, wrists and fingertips do most of the work on the shot and the arm follows straight through after the shot.

The wrist should be locked, that is, not turning to the left or right. The wrist and fingers are really what control the shot more than anything else. Don't follow the flight of the ball when it's released. Use the free hand simply as a guide, so that it is not interfering with the shot. You should feel comfortable shooting the jump shot.

Once a young player has those fundamentals down, I like to take him close to the basket and work on him shooting the ball, getting a good touch, shooting a good, soft shot and getting a good backspin on the ball, without exaggerating the backspin. The way to get that backspin is to be sure the last thing that touches the ball are the three middle fingers.

After that, it's up to the youngster. He must practice all those things until he feels himself tiring, then quit and go to something else and finally come back to shooting again.

When you have perfected your jump shot and you begin to use it in a game, it is imperative that you always have absolute concentration, eyes glued on the basket so that nothing disturbs you—the yelling of the crowd, a defensive man's hand in your face, any movement on the floor.

All the great shooters have absolute concentration, but when it comes to concentration on the jumper, Jerry West is in a class by himself. He has the greatest concentration I've ever seen on the jump shot. When Jerry goes up for a shot, anything can happen—the building can be falling down—but Jerry won't let it break his concentration.

I can't overemphasize the importance of practice. Keeping your touch on your jump shot is almost like a professional golfer keeping his putting touch. The only way to maintain that touch is by constant practice. I want to get my jump

Like all good jump shooters, Elgin Baylor releases the ball off the middle fingers. *(Malcolm W. Emmons)*

shot to the point where I can get up at four in the morning and make it. Sam Jones used to call his jumper money in the bank. That's how I feel. My jump shot is my bread and butter.

Just as important as shooting it right is being able to shoot it at all. That is, for it to do any good, you have to be able to get the shot off. You can be the greatest shooter in the world in practice, but if you can't get the shot off in a game, it doesn't matter how great a shooter you are. So you have to learn to get it off quickly. If you see the opening, shoot, because that opening is not going to be there a split second later.

In that regard, range is extremely important. Take Oscar Robertson, for example. If you give him an 18-foot shot, he'll try to get a 15-foot shot. Why? One word: percentage. You always have to try to get the percentage working for you. That's why the dunk is such a great shot. Wilt Chamberlain once made thirty-six straight dunks. That's what I call percentage.

I always try to pick my range on my jumper, but there are some nights when I feel it going that I can go outside my range and still make them.

You can't keep changing the way you shoot your jumper. You've got to release the ball the same way all the time. I try to get a lot of spin on my shot. To repeat, my fingertips are last to touch the ball, my eyes are on the basket, my forearm, wrist and fingers are in line.

When I shoot a ball and I feel that I shot it well, I know I've controlled the ball. The jump shot isn't meant to be shot from a height of 3 or 4 feet off the floor. If you can jump off the floor that high and still shoot comfortably, by all means do it. But it's not necessary.

Players vary on when they release the ball. Most of them will shoot at the peak of their jump. Elvin Hayes of San Diego is a good example of a great jump shooter who releases the ball at the peak of his jump.

But there are other great shooters who release the ball on the way up or on the way down. Kevin Loughery of the

Billy Cunningham shoots the jumper on his downward flight. *(Malcolm W. Emmons)*

Bullets releases the ball on his upward flight. With his quick release, Kevin found that was the best way for him to shoot to fool the defense.

Elgin Baylor, one of the greatest jump shooters I've ever seen, often shoots the ball on his way down. Billy Cunningham of Philadelphia is another player who jumps as high as he can, then starts his downward flight and shoots the ball on his way down.

I don't know why a player releases the ball when he does. These are just things that they have perfected. You do what comes naturally, what is most comfortable and what you've been most successful with. Most players start out shooting the jumper at the peak of their jump, then change somewhere along the way. The important thing is that you shoot the same way all the time. You shouldn't shoot one way in practice and another way in the game, just as in practice you shouldn't shoot outside the range you will use in the game.

Some nights I've seen players shoot the ball and do it successfully even though they violate all the rules. That may be all right on some nights, but over a period of years the great shooters are going to be the ones whose fundamentals are correct. No matter how they jump or what they do with their legs, they all have the same way of releasing the ball.

A perfect example is my teammate, Dick Barnett. Dick is one of the great jump shooters in the NBA, but he has a crazy way of shooting. His legs are tucked up underneath his body and he looks very awkward. Somebody once described him as looking like an inverted question mark. When you see him, you think, "There's no way a guy can shoot like that."

The truth is that Barnett is really doing everything by the book. The legs have no importance in the shot. From the waist up, he's doing it the way all great shooters do it. To him, that's a comfortable position. I assume he developed that style when he was young and not very strong and shooting the ball was a strain on him. He probably started kicking his legs like that to try to get more force on the ball.

You see youngsters do a lot of crazy things with their legs

when they shoot because they don't have the strength, and that was probably the case with Barnett. He developed a habit that stayed with him. But his shot is really all wrist. His hands and fingertips are doing all the work; the position of his legs means nothing. If you take ten great shooters, they may have ten different ways of shooting the ball and they may all look different. But where it counts, in the forearm, wrist and fingertips, they're all doing things by the book.

Very often youngsters ask me where I aim when I shoot the jumper. That, too, varies with individuals, but my way is to imagine there is a big cylinder there and I want to shoot the ball and have it go over the rim and drop into the middle of that cylinder. I aim for the middle of the basket; it's like flipping a piece of paper into a trash can.

The arc of the shot is important. It shouldn't be too exaggerated an arc and not too straight, although there have been some very good shooters who were line-drive shooters. Tom Heinsohn of the Celtics was very successful with a line-drive shot, and Cazzie Russell shoots a line drive, but most players can't shoot that way. If you throw it on a line, there is much less margin for error.

I've been able to steal a few baskets because of my soft touch and medium arc. Sometimes I'll get lucky and I'll be at half court, on my way back to my defensive position, when the ball will finally drop through. That's the advantage of a soft touch and a medium arc. The hard line drive will either bang in or hit the rim hard and bounce away. The soft shot is more likely to bounce around the rim, and sometimes you get a lucky bounce.

There are few shooters around the NBA who are good with the backboard. John Havlicek of the Celtics is one. And Sam Jones, a former Celtic, was another great backboard shooter, great at banking his jumper. Basically, though, the backboard is not an essential thing for jump shooters. Most of them aim for the rim and the nets.

Although I preferred to play center, my being switched to forward when Walt Bellamy joined the team wasn't all bad. My scoring average dropped to 15.5, but I made the All-Star team as a forward. Also, playing the forward position for three seasons helped make me a better center. I guess I do more things like a forward than any other center in the league—shooting facing the basket, moving outside for a shot, driving to the hoop. I still have a touch of forward in me. I guess I always will.

Red Holzman treats his players like men, not boys. *(United Press International Photo)*

5
A Dollar a Minute

The first phase in the making of a championship for the New York Knickerbockers came on December 27, 1967. On that date, with their record an unsatisfactory 6–13, the Knicks got a new coach. William (Red) Holzman, a native of New York who had played his college ball under the legendary Nat Holman at CCNY and his pro ball with the Rochester Royals and who had coached the Milwaukee Hawks a decade before, was named to replace Dick McGuire.

In less than four seasons as a pro, Willis Reed was playing for his fourth coach.

In all, Willis Reed has played for six coaches—Lendon Stone in high school, Fred Hobdy at Grambling, and the four Knick coaches, Eddie Donovan, Harry Gallatin, Dick McGuire and Red Holzman.

Each of the six coaches in my basketball life made some contribution to my career, but when I think of my coach, I think of Lendon Stone. I have to say he was the most important. Not that he was the best coach or the most helpful, but he was the first. I do not mean to slight any of the other five, but if it hadn't been for Coach Stone, there would never have been a Coach Hobdy or a Coach Holzman for me.

Coach Stone found me, encouraged me to play basketball and developed me to the point where I was able to take advantage of my natural assets—my height and my shooting touch. Without him, I never would have been a basketball player, I never would have gone to college to play basketball and therefore I never would have been a pro.

He is the reason I believe the beginning of a basketball player's career is so important. It's like the beginning a child has when he comes into the world. When he grows up, the two people he has to be most grateful to are his parents. If it wasn't for them, he would be nothing. The same is true in sports, in a manner of speaking. The first teacher is always the most important because he determines if there will ever be a second teacher. More than one potential athlete's career was destroyed before it got started by a poor first teacher.

Coach Stone is the man who saw this kid and took time out to help him when he could have been home with his family. He's the man who took a nothing and made him into some kind of ballplayer.

Coach Hobdy was important, too, because he gave me the chance to play college ball and because the style of ball he played at Grambling taught me the value of hard work and training. He prepared me for what I was going to experience as a pro. He had been a center at Grambling, too, and is a big, strong man who speaks softly most of the time, but commands respect when he speaks. He has been particularly successful developing big men.

I owe a lot to Coach Hobdy's jumping drills, which helped me develop the coordination and the rebounding skills that were going to be so important to me in the pros.

The basic difference between a coach in high school or college and a professional coach is that the high school and college coach has to be more of a teacher than the professional coach. There is very little teaching required of a pro coach. His main job is handling players. He's got to be capable of dealing with professional athletes, and there is no formula for dealing with pro athletes. Some get the job done with kindness, others have to be tough; but it all comes down to having the kind of personality that can deal with twelve other personalities, or twenty-five personalities in baseball, or forty personalities in football.

Just about everybody who gets to be a coach in the NBA knows the game of basketball inside out. But it takes more than knowledge of the game to win championships. If all coaches are pretty much equal in their knowledge and their ability to impart and implement that knowledge, why do some coaches win and others lose?

The main reason is the players. It's an old saying in sports but a true one: "You have to have the horses." You can be the greatest coach in the world, but if you don't have the material, you're not going to win. You might beat somebody with your coaching, you might even win ten games a season with your coaching, although I'm probably being too generous. Don't get me wrong, the coach is important, but if it comes down to winning a championship, the coach is not as important as the players. A good coach with bad players won't win, but a bad coach with good players will win sometime.

My first pro coach was Eddie Donovan and you couldn't find a finer man in all the world. He was like a father to me, just as Coach Stone and Coach Hobdy were. These three men, Coach Stone, Coach Hobdy and Coach Donovan, have been the greatest inspirations in my life.

Eddie Donovan did so much for me. As a coach, he was helpful, kind, patient and understanding. As a general manager, he was generous and considerate. I consider him a friend and I think so much of him there is just nothing in this world he could ask me to do that I wouldn't do. He's a beautiful man.

It's impossible for me to evaluate Donovan as a coach because I didn't play for him very long. There was no question that he knew basketball. He has one of the greatest basketball minds you'll ever find, but right there is an example of a great coach not having the horses. You never knew what was going to happen that first year. We just didn't have the talent to win for Eddie, but he was the kind of guy you played your heart out for. It used to hurt me when we lost while Eddie was coaching. I knew it also hurt him.

And I wanted to win because I knew he'd lose his job if we kept losing. I didn't want that to happen because I liked him and I knew he was a good coach. It wasn't his fault we were losing. It's one of the ironies of sports that here was a good coach, a coach who was well liked by his players, and as hard as we played for him, we just couldn't win. We simply didn't have the talent.

After thirty-eight games in my rookie season, the inevitable happened—Donovan was replaced by Harry Gallatin. He was more of a disciplinarian than Donovan, but I never had any trouble with him. Maybe it was because I had played for a tough coach in college and was used to discipline.

A lot of the guys didn't like Harry. I guess it was natural, in a way, because he replaced a man everybody liked. We were annoyed with ourselves for not being able to win for Eddie and we were disappointed when he was replaced. We hated to see him go, so anybody who came in had two strikes against him from the start. It was more than that with Harry. He was tough and demanding and he was cold and aloof. We figured that someone who had played in the league and had been a star for so many years would understand players a little more. Harry didn't seem to understand us at all. He didn't know how to treat his players. He acted as if he didn't trust us to be on our own and he treated us like kids, not like grown men and professional athletes. A lot of the players resented being treated like that.

Personally, I liked Harry as a man. I didn't think he was the greatest coach I ever played for—but, on the other hand, we weren't exactly the greatest players he ever saw either.

Dick McGuire took over after we had played twenty-one

games in my second year. I thought Dickie was a great guy to play for. He treated you like a man. A lot of people said he couldn't communicate, but I didn't find that to be true. And I still consider him one of my good friends. He certainly knew all there was to know about the game. I'm just sorry we couldn't win for him. He's the kind of guy, like Donovan, that you hate to lose for.

After thirty-seven games of the 1967–68 season, Dickie was replaced by Red Holzman. I have to believe that the timing was just perfect for Red. We were starting to get better. Walt Frazier was coming of age, Bill Bradley was adjusting to the league and we got Dave DeBusschere from Detroit. We were going to do the job. With the kind of team we had, we would have to have had a very bad coach *not* to win. Maybe we would have won a championship if McGuire or Gallatin or Donovan had still been the coach. But we'll never know.

Still, that doesn't take any credit away from Red. He won. He went all the way to a championship, and you can't ask any more than that from any coach.

The biggest thing that Red brought to the job was something I mentioned earlier: the kind of personality that made him capable of handling players. The first thing he said when he became coach was:

"You guys are men and that's the way I'm going to treat you. You know how to take care of yourselves. You know what you can do and what you can't do. There will be no curfew. I don't even want to see you until game time. Your performance is the only thing that counts. Do your job, play ball and we won't have any problems."

All the guys appreciated that. And I don't think any of us abuses the privilege. If a ballplayer has pride, he's not going to let his outside activities interfere with his professional career.

It may seem surprising that a coach has to remind a player to take care of his body. You would think that a professional athlete would realize that his career depends on his body and that he would do anything to take care of it. But you'd be surprised how many players throw away great careers by not taking care of themselves. It seems to be the fashion lately for athletes not only to abuse their bodies but to boast about it in books or magazine articles.

Personally, I just can't see that kind of thing. Let's not even talk about the image you're supposed to project to youngsters. That's important, but let's be selfish about it. Let's talk about the player's career. I take the view that I'm a man in business. My business is playing basketball. And the main asset I have in my business is my body. Take that away from me and I've got nothing. I've got only a few years to get myself financially comfortable, and I'd be a fool to give up any of those years by abusing my body and shortening my career.

Basketball, especially, demands a very great deal of a man physically, night in and night out. In order for your body to produce for you, you've got to take care of your body. You can't drink and stay out late and burn the candle at both ends and expect to produce at maximum efficiency. If you do those things, you're hurting yourself and you're hurting a lot of other people—your teammates, your family, the fans who come to see you give your best.

Despite all you hear and read about athletes abusing their bodies, staying out late, drinking and carrying on and boasting about it, I believe those people are the exception. Most athletes are conscious of their bodies. I would say that most athletes, especially the great ones, are completely dedicated to the game. Players like Oscar Robertson, Jerry West, Dick Barnett, have complete dedication. They live, eat and sleep basketball. Wes Unseld is another player who has total devotion to the game. And there are many more. In fact, they're in the majority.

Quite a few players do let themselves get so involved in outside activities—endorsements and businesses and things —that they let their main business suffer. I think it's great for an athlete to make money in outside activities, especially if he is building for the future, so he'll have something when he can no longer play ball. I'm involved in several outside projects myself. But I try never to let them interfere with basketball. I keep reminding myself that, without basketball, I wouldn't have these other activities.

So, Red Holzman came in and treated us like men and we won a championship. But Red would be the first to admit that it was a united effort between players and coach, each man doing his share. Red deserves a lot of credit. I've seen him make many moves with reference to a play or a substitution or an adjustment that made the difference in winning a game. And I've also seen him get up in front of the team before a game, hold up a long piece of paper with his game plan and a lot of diagrams and plays on it and say, "Everything on this paper is useless if you guys don't go out and make it work."

Red is a funny little guy. He's full of strange expressions and sayings—homilies, I guess you would call them. Things like "Never get your hair cut by a bald-headed barber; he has no respect for your hair," and, "Never take medical advice from a waiter."

To someone from Louisiana, Red looks and sounds like the typical New Yorker. He's a conservative dresser, especially when you see him in the mod world of the players on his team. He always seems to have a cigar in his mouth, and he'll point the cigar when he talks. With that cigar and the way he talks and walks, kind of hunched over a little, I can't help thinking that he reminds me of Groucho Marx.

I must say for Red that he never takes himself seriously to the point that he believes he's indispensable or that he won the championship, not us. You have to have both a coach making the right moves at the right time and the players carrying out those moves.

Sometimes we'll lose a tough game, and Red and I will talk about it and he'll say, "Maybe if I had done it this way from the start we might have won." What can you say? He works hard at his part of the game and I work hard at my part. His job is to make sure that he tries to put the right players in at the right time and to keep the team flowing as a unit, with everybody doing his job.

I've often heard him say that the men he has to worry about most are the ones who are not playing, not the ones who are.

"I've got to keep these guys on the bench happy," he says. "They're the most important guys. You who are playing are going to be happy. But here are these guys on the bench with a lot of talent and they're not playing. I've got to keep them happy, keep them mentally ready to play, keep them feeling like part of the team."

It's a good philosophy, and he's absolutely right. We have players on the bench who were always starters in high school and college—not only starters but stars, All-Americans most of them. They could be regulars on other teams, but here they are subs and they'll play maybe five minutes a game. It's the coach's job to keep them ready so that when they play those five minutes, they're able to make a contribution to the team.

Red and I have had our differences. In the early days when he had to make an example of someone to establish his authority, he'd use me. I had a feeling he was picking on me unnecessarily, getting on me for some error I made on the court. I was hurt. Here I am doing my job, I thought, and he knows I'm doing my job, but he still gets on me. That bothered me. It took me a while to understand what he was trying to do. Since I was the center and captain, the biggest man on the team, he was using me as an example that he was not going to play favorites. In other words, he wanted the guys to feel, that if he could raise hell with Willis, he could do it with anybody. I had to learn this and now I can see it was a good thing for team morale, although at the time I felt that he was picking on me unnecessarily.

The only thing Red is concerned with is winning games, not a popularity contest. I think he likes all the guys on the team, but I don't think he would ever do anything to let his personal feelings interfere with what he believes is best for the ball club.

Aside from handling men, a coach's biggest job is making match-ups, substitutions and knowing when to call a time out to make an adjustment or slow the opposition's momentum. As far as strategy goes, Red concentrates most of his effort on the defense and lets the offense pretty much take care of itself. Most of the plays we run are fairly basic anyway. Bradley, DeBusschere or Barnett will come up with a lot of the plays we run. Red doesn't care. Some coaches don't want the players to take over like that, but Red's feeling is if it can help the team, let's try it and see what it looks like.

Red is very good at keeping the guys loose. He'll come into the dressing room before a game and hold up a single piece of paper in one hand and a batch of papers in the other hand.

"Clyde," he'll say to Frazier, "these are for you. These are all the things you're doing wrong."

Red likes to kid with Frazier. During the game he's always on him to get back on defense. One game he kept yelling: "Clyde, get back on defense. Back, Clyde, back. Clyde, where the hell are you?"

"Here I am, Red," said Frazier, sitting right next to Red on the bench.

Another thing about Red is that he is a fanatic about punctuality. He hates to see a guy late for anything. When we're on the road and we have to take a bus to the arena, if Red says the bus leaves at 6 P.M., we'd better be there by 6 P.M. He has a big, old-fashioned pocket watch which he pulls out and being late costs you a dollar a minute.

Once, just as the bus was about to leave, Frazier jumped out and yelled, "Hold the bus for me, Red, I'll be right back."

"It'll cost you, Clyde," Red said.

When Frazier came back ten minutes later, he was carrying a pair of new shoes he'd left at the hotel.

"That will cost you ten dollars," Red said.

"That's all right, Red," Frazier said. "These shoes cost me a hundred dollars. So I saved ninety dollars."

Things like this have helped keep the Knicks close, and Red Holzman has a lot to do with it. Of course, winning is good for morale, too, and the credit for that must go to the entire organization.

When Eddie Donovan was replaced as coach, he was made general manager and he had a lot to do with building the Knicks into a winning team. Holzman was the chief scout at the time and most of what the Knicks have become is a result of the draft.

They didn't just go out and try to get the best players they could get. They got players who could play as a team, like a machine, every gear having a different function. It's no accident that the Knicks have players who work well together; it was by design. It goes beyond talent. It goes with the type of men they are, with each one's personality and character.

When Donovan and Holzman were picking players, they looked for one special characteristic. They chose players who were concerned with just one thing: winning.

You have to have a coach who makes the right move at the right time. *(United Press International Photo)*

I was happy to be back at center. *(United Press International Photo)*

6
The Thing to Remember

The telephone rang in the suburban Detroit home of the Pistons' forward Dave DeBusschere in the early evening of December 19, 1968. The man of the house climbed down from a ladder to answer the phone. He had been hanging a picture.

The voice on the other end of the wire belonged to Ed Coil, General Manager of the Pistons.

"Dave," said Coil, "we've traded you to the Knicks for Walt Bellamy and Howard Komives. I'm sorry I couldn't tell you in person, but there wasn't time. The deal was just made."

The trade has been called—not infrequently and not incorrectly—the making of the Knicks.

There are many reasons why the addition of Dave DeBusschere constituted the making of the Knicks. Not the least of those reasons was apparent on December 20, 1968, when the Knicks lined up for the start of a game with the Pistons. The starting lineup for the Knicks that night was as follows: Walt Frazier and Dick Barnett, guards; Dave DeBusschere and Bill Bradley, forwards; Willis Reed, center.

It wasn't that I was happy to see Bellamy go; you never like to see a teammate get traded. But I was happy with the trade because it meant I would again be playing center, the position in which I was more comfortable, more confident and, I believe, more capable.

I knew it would be a lot easier getting reacquainted with my old position than it would be to try to learn the moves of a new position.

Playing forward for three years had been a big break. I learned how to maneuver for my shot and I really perfected my jump shot. The most important shot for a center is the jumper because there are so many variations off the jump shot that you can use.

First, I think I have an advantage in being left-handed. Most of the centers I play against are not accustomed to playing against a left-hander. The same is true in baseball. As a rule, right-handed hitters can hit right-handed pitchers better than left-handed hitters can hit left-handed pitchers. That's because there are fewer left-handed than right-handed pitchers, and the same is true in basketball; there are more right-handed than left-handed centers.

I'm a left-handed shooter 99 per cent of the time. The other 1 per cent is when I get into a position where I have to shoot right-handed. I believe that when you start playing, you should spend all your time doing things with one hand, your natural way, until you've come to the point where you feel you have perfected that skill sufficiently to begin working on the other hand.

There is no such thing in basketball as a jack-of-all-trades or a completely ambidextrous ballplayer. If a player is a natural right-hander and he dribbles and shoots right-handed, he's always going to be better with his right hand no matter how much he practices with his left. Very few players use their left and right hands equally well. It's just not possible.

Even though I'm left-handed, I like to turn to my left out of the pivot on the jumper. That means I'm shooting my shot right up in my opponent's face. A lot of people think I would

On the hook shot the ball rests in your hand, and the wrist and fingertips are used as in the jumper. *(Farrell* and *Peter Hollander)*

get my shots blocked, but I don't. I turn to my left because I like to have my shooting hand as close to the basket as I possibly can. I don't worry about getting my shots blocked. I've had success turning to my left out of the pivot, so I'll just keep right on doing it that way until I see a reason to change.

I said before that the jump shot out of the pivot allows you to use so many variations. You can dribble left and turn left or dribble left and turn right. And you can do the opposite: dribble right and turn in either direction. Also you can vary the amount of times you dribble the ball before you go up with the shot . . . one dribble, two dribbles, three or four. Although I believe in keeping the ball on the move, I think, for a center, the ball should be dribbled no more than four times. Generally, one or two dribbles are plenty, especially if you're in traffic; then you don't want to put the ball on the floor too often because each time you do you're in danger of having it taken away from you.

Another thing you can do to vary the pace is, after the dribble, fake with your head, arm or shoulders to get the defensive man to commit himself. I use a lot of fakes. It's something I worked on from the time I was in college.

When I got to Grambling I couldn't execute a head fake. Coach Hobdy showed me how to do it, and once I learned, I kept doing it and kept getting better at it. In our league, every little thing you can pick up is important. When you reach the pros, there isn't too much difference between you and the man playing against you, and the only difference may be something you do, not something great, but some little thing like a head fake. A lot of times I can throw the defensive man's timing off just a little bit and go up for the shot.

Years ago, every center used the hook shot as his greatest weapon. Today, it's rare to see more than one or two hook shots from a center in a game. I use it, but only on occasion. On the hook shot, the ball is not held, it's just resting in your hand and it's shot with a hooking motion from behind you. You still use the fingertips and wrist as you do with the jump shot, however.

The problem with the hook shot is that once you decide to hook, you have no choice, you have to go through with it. On the jumper, I can go up in the air and if I'm blocked or if I see a teammate free under the basket, I can still pass the ball off to him. That's why I look for the jump shot, and I generally take more jumpers in a game than any other shot.

As a center, it's not vital to have good range on your shots, but you have to shoot the ball on the move, going to the basket, moving across the keyhole. My basic responsibility lies close to the basket. You should be able to make 60 per cent of your shots around the basket, but your percentage is going to lie in whether you're taking the good shot or the bad one. If I've got a chance to score, I always go with my best shot and my best hand, unless there's a situation where I can't go with my best hand.

On layups, I try to use my body for protection. The book says you should go off your right foot to make a right-handed layup and off your left foot to make a left-handed layup. That's the right way, but if you watch the pros, you'll see that they often disobey the book. They can do it because they've got such great balance, but for a youngster just starting out, or even a high school player, it's best to follow the book. There's nothing as embarrassing as missing a layup when you're in there all alone. Even the greatest pros miss them, but it's rare.

I try to always play to my strength. If I have a choice, I'll try to make my layups from the left side and I'll use the backboard. When I go up the middle, I use the rim. Only under the basket will I contest the defensive man, and I'll let the rim and the net play defense for me on the reverse layup. I like to go under the basket on my layup because I think it gives me added protection. It's the safest way, and I always like to be sure.

As a center, I'm also the hub of the offense. That means the ball comes into me and many of the plays revolve around me. I have to be sure to keep the ball moving and to give the ball off to players cutting off me. If a teammate is cutting, the pass can be just a flip or shovel. At all other times, the

In these four pictures I demonstrate the proper technique on a layup out of the pivot. The defender is one of my former coaches, Howard Willis. *(Farrell)*

The rim and net play defense for me on the reverse layup. *(United Press International Photo)*

pass should be quick and hard, usually tossed from the chest with two hands and with the wrist doing most of the work.

Sometimes, after I take a defensive rebound, I have to throw a pass down court. The best pass to use then is the baseball pass, which is exactly what it sounds like—a pass tossed overhand as you would throw a baseball.

I purposely omit the dunk shot here because I believe it's part of rebounding, and those subjects will be discussed in Chapter 8.

There is one thing that is true of all shots, no matter what the shot is—a hook, jumper or simple layup. The thing to remember above everything else is: Never take any shot, not even the simplest shot, for granted.

The chest pass. *(Farrell)*

The bounce pass. *(Farrell)*

The overhead pass. *(Farrell)*

The baseball pass. *(Farrell)*

Walt Frazier has ice water in his veins on the foul line. *(Malcolm W. Emmons)*

7

On the Line

Willis Reed has never led the NBA in foul shooting, but then few big men have. What is more important, Reed has never hurt the Knicks on the foul line, but then many big men have.

His excellent, naturally soft shooting touch has made Reed a better-than-average free-throw shooter, especially for a big man. In his career as a Knick, Reed has averaged almost 75 per cent from the foul line. That means that of every four free throws he has taken as a Knick—and he has shot over three thousand—Reed makes three of them.

Foul shooting is something that is taken too lightly in basketball, but it shouldn't be because it's a vital part of the game. I guess you can compare it with putting in golf, the sacrifice bunt in baseball and blocking in football. These are the little things, the underrated things that are the difference between winning and losing.

Many games are won or lost on the foul line. If you play

Shooting fouls: take a deep breath to relax, get the feel of the ball, and the rest is just like the jumper—except that the feet don't leave the ground. *(Farrell)*

basketball, it's very likely that one night, in some little gym
in Somewhere, U.S.A., you're going to step to the foul line
with one second remaining and the whole game depending
on you. Then the burden of proof will be on your shoulders
and you'll show what you're made of.

When we won our record-breaking eighteenth game in a
row, Walt Frazier stepped to the line and, with ice water in
his veins, made two foul shots to win the game. Lew Alcindor missed two fouls against us in the second game of the
Eastern final playoffs in 1970 that could have beaten us.
In the same game, Cazzie Russell walked to the line and
made two important fouls late in the game under great
pressure.

As it turned out, we won that game by 1 point and, who
knows, if Alcindor had made his two shots or Cazzie hadn't
made his, we may never have won the championship.

Basketball is a game of mistakes. When a guy makes a
mistake, he must learn to recover from it. A lot of guys will
be finished for the night. Some guys will come back, as
Cazzie did that night against Milwaukee. He had missed an
easy layup earlier, but he didn't get down. He came back
and made those fouls.

When I go to the foul line, I always take my time. I take
a deep breath and I bounce the ball quite a few times. The
deep breath and the bouncing of the ball serve two purposes: it helps me relax and it gives me a rest. It also gives
my teammates a rest.

I won't let the ball go until I'm relaxed and ready to shoot.
I spin the ball in my hand until I get the feel of the ball I
want. Then I concentrate on the basket, and the foul shot is
like the jump shot except, of course, that my feet don't leave
the ground. The ball is thrown with the wrists and fingertips,
just like the jumper, with the middle three fingers the last
to touch the ball, giving me that little backspin I want to
ensure a soft shot.

A lot of attention has been given, through the years, to
Wilt Chamberlain's problems on the foul line. People are
always asking me why Wilt isn't a better foul shooter and I

have no answer for them, except that it has probably become a psychological thing with him, a mental block, now.

Then, again, maybe that's just his weakness in the game. I guess one is entitled to have one weakness, especially when he can do as many things as well as Wilt can.

Rebounding against Wes Unseld. *(United Press International Photo)*

8
"You're the Only One Who Can . . ."

In his rookie season as a pro, Willis Reed grabbed 1,175 rebounds. It was more than any New York Knick had pulled down in any of the previous eighteen years of the team's history.

Four years later the record was broken—by Reed, as he took down 1,191 rebounds in the 1968–69 season.

The following year he passed the career record for a Knick, the 5,935 recoveries taken by Harry Gallatin, Reed's second professional coach.

Only once, in his troubled second season when he switched from center to forward, has Willis Reed failed to grab at least 1,000 rebounds in any pro season. And, in the fifth game of the 1969–70 preliminary playoff with the Bullets, he added another Knick rebound record with 36.

The thing that always seemed to set me apart and put me in a special classification when I was in high school was that I was the only kid who could dunk the ball. A few of the other kids could jump up and touch the rim, and trying to do that one day, they bent the rim.

The dunk is the surest way to two points. *(Farrell)*

When Coach Stone saw the bent rim, he blamed me. He wouldn't listen to me when I denied being responsible.

"I know it's you," he argued, "because you're the only one who can dunk the ball."

There was one other time when my ability to dunk got me in trouble with Coach Stone. It was in the ninth grade and I was playing basketball with a few of my friends. We used to play in a wide-open field, with the basketball courts behind the baseball diamond, and you would have to walk through the baseball field to get to the basketball courts.

This particular day a lot of kids tried to dunk the ball and they couldn't do it, so they asked me to dunk. I refused. Then they started goading me, calling me chicken and all. Now I was challenged. I said I'd show those guys. I took the ball and dunked it.

Just as I did, Coach Stone walked into the park. He came just in time to see me dunk and he raised hell.

"You can't even hold a basketball," he said, "you can't even catch a basketball, you can't even run up and down the court and here you are showing off, dunking the ball.

"That's not going to make you a basketball player," he continued. "You're going to have to do all the other things before you start dunking."

He really put me down. He made me feel very small and, of course, he was absolutely right. Nowadays, when a kid gets to be pretty tall, the first thing he thinks about is dunking the ball, and it's not that important. At least it's not important until you have perfected all the other fundamental skills.

Even though I agree with Coach Stone that dunking is not important until you have learned the other basic skills of the game of basketball, I find it hard to agree with the rules committee in banning the dunk in high school and college. If a kid can dunk the ball, I think he should. I don't see anything wrong with it. Dunking the ball is an incentive for a young player to jump.

You see a little player like Calvin Murphy, only 5 feet, 10 inches, and he can dunk, one hand, two hands, reverse. It

You don't have to be a great jumper to be a great rebounder, as Bailey Howell has proved. *(United Press International Photo)*

adds something to the game. The fan loves to see a little guy —or even a big guy—dunk the ball.

Generally, a ball club that has four or five players who can dunk will be a good rebounding team.

It's not necessarily true that the ability to jump is something you're born with. You can teach a boy to jump, give him jumping drills, make him practice dunking, have him skip rope for balance.

There is a right way to jump and a wrong way. You should spring off the balls of your feet, and it must be a strong upward surge all of a sudden, as violent as possible, with as much force as possible. You should practice not running several steps and jumping but taking one step before jumping.

Once you have worked on that, a good way to practice is just jumping straight up and down, over and over. Balance is important because in rebounding, jumping is not the only skill required. There are others, like timing. A lot of great jumpers are not great rebounders. People will see a guy get all the way up and they will say, "Oh-h, can he jump!" He may be able to jump, but the important question is: "Can he rebound?"

Bailey Howell was not a great jumper, but he was a great rebounder, especially on the offensive board. He had great timing. He had the sense of being able to get the ball at the peak of his jump. It does a player no good to jump 3 feet in the air if he's going to get the ball when he's at 2 feet.

Jerry Lucas has the ability of knowing where the ball is going to come off on the rebound, like a good outfielder who can sense where the ball is going to land as soon as it's hit, and goes back and gets a good jump on the ball.

Nate Thurmond and Wes Unseld have the knack of looking at a shot going up, and figuring the angle and judging where the rebound is going to be. That's a talent, but it can be acquired with experience and practice.

Obviously, it's always best to try to rebound with two hands, but it's not always possible. If there's a choice, on the offensive board, I try to go up and get the ball with two

Wes gets his share. *(United Press International Photo)*

hands; then while I'm up in the air with the ball in my hands I make my split-second judgment on whether to go to the hoop or come back down and then go up again.

If it's clear that I don't have much of a chance to grab it with two hands, I try to go up and get at least a piece of the ball to keep it alive. I'll try either to tap it toward the basket or just tap it anywhere and hope that DeBusschere or Bradley is in position to control the ball for us.

A lot of the skill of rebounding is a learning process. If you really concentrate and develop good depth perception, you can become a better rebounder. For example, knowing the shooters is important. If there are hard shooters, the ball will have a tendency to rebound one way, and if there are soft shooters, it will rebound another way. Therefore, it is necessary to study the shooters, not only those on your team, but those on the other team as well.

Some players are long shooters. By that I mean that when they miss they usually overshoot the basket. The short shooters usually miss in front of the basket. Dick Barnett likes to shoot coming down the right corner, and if he misses, the ball usually comes back to him or goes over the basket. Dave DeBusschere is a hard shooter, and his shot has more of a rebound to it than Barnett's or Bill Bradley's. They are both soft shooters.

Study these things and one day it will pay off for you. These are the little things that may be the difference between a player averaging 17 rebounds a game and one averaging 20 rebounds a game.

You just don't become a great rebounder all of a sudden. There are no short-cuts and no gimmicks that will help you. This is something you work at and work at, and some players are more gifted at it than others. Bill Russell is an example. He was a great defensive player and a great rebounder with unbelievable timing and coordination. But he just was not an outstanding shooter.

You would figure that a man with his timing and coordination would be a great shooter, but he wasn't. Watching Bill, you knew he would never be a great shooter. Probably if he

I try to grab rebounds with two hands. *(Farrell)*

Sometimes I have to take the rebound with one hand. *(Farrell)*

had worked more on his offensive game, he could have been a better shooter. But then maybe his defensive game wouldn't have been as good.

I don't think you can ever find one ballplayer who can score 50 points a night and block as many shots as Russell and get as many rebounds as Chamberlain. It's impossible, although if any one player ever came closest to doing all that, it would have to be Wilt Chamberlain.

Bill Russell set the standard for defense. *(United Press International Photo)*

9

"I Haven't Found Him Yet"

Bill Russell of the Boston Celtics had led the defensive revolution in the NBA. Nobody played defense like Russell, but many tried, imitating his free-wheeling, intimidating style, and defense was improving all over the league.

When the famed "Eagle with the Beard" retired before the 1969–70 season, every center in the league tried to move in to assume Russell's role as the defensive menace in the NBA. It's axiomatic that you don't win in the NBA without a good big man and that the team with the best big man will probably win everything.

Of all the potential successors to Russell's defensive throne, one stood above the rest. He had started playing basketball in a small Louisiana town the year Bill Russell joined the Boston Celtics. Like Russell, he was left-handed, and he became the acknowledged successor to Russell when he took the great Celtic's place on the NBA All-Defensive team.

For years, Willis Reed had tried to pattern his game after his idol, Bill Russell. Now he was considered to be Russell's successor.

113

But if getting to that position of eminence was difficult, staying there was going to be doubly difficult.

My old roommate, Bill Hosket, used to have a little sign pinned to his locker in the Knick dressing room. It said DESIRE PLUS DEFENSE EQUALS SUCCESS.

I guess you could say that slogan became the trademark of the 1969–70 Knicks. Defense wins games. I think we proved that in the 1969–70 season. We allowed the fewest points of any team in the league and we won the championship. You don't need any more proof than that.

The Knicks are a team dedicated to defense. We know we'll score our points, but we work at keeping the other team from scoring. When we are out on the court, we are five guys working together, all with one common goal, and we are always helping one another out on defense.

This is the philosophy of team defense taught by Eddie Donovan and Red Holzman, a philosophy based on the thought that somebody might make a mistake out there and if he does, somebody else is going to have to pick him up. It's the only way to play in the NBA because these are the best basketball players in the world and they can do amazing things with a basketball. One-on-one, they're going to kill you.

I think the days are gone when one man will score 100 points in a game, as Wilt Chamberlain did some years ago. I don't even believe you'll ever see a man score in the 70's again. There are players who are capable of doing it, but they won't.

The reason I think they won't is . . . well, actually, there are two reasons. The first reason is the defense in the league, which has improved and is getting better every year. The second reason is that nobody is going to get that many shots in a game. Every team in the league has five players who can score and they realize a balanced attack is more important than having one man do all the scoring. It's much easier to stop a team when one or two or even three men are doing all the scoring than it is when all five out there can put the

Lew Alcindor is tough to stop in close. *(Vernon J. Biever Photo)*

I spread out on defense to make the biggest obstacle I can. *(Farrell)*

I like to change the angle on my man to avoid falling into a pattern on defense. *(Farrell)*

ball in the hoop. What it comes down to is: I'd rather score 20 points and win than score 30 points and lose.

You don't stop players like Chamberlain, Alcindor, Robertson or West. Those guys are going to get their points. You have to try to stop the other guys on the team. If a player averages 8 points a game and he gets 16 against you, that's 100 per cent improvement and that's the guy who beats you, the guy who doubles his average.

The Knicks are successful because even though we are not a great rebounding team and are outrebounded almost every time we play, we compensate for it by our defense. Our aggressive defense, especially by Walt Frazier, forces our opponents into a lot of turnovers on steals, and these turnovers result in fast breaks where we get easy layups or open shots. I repeat, defense wins games because it forces mistakes, and the team that makes the fewest mistakes is usually the team that wins.

You can't really teach an individual to play defense. You can help him, give him tips, correct errors he makes, but you can't teach him how to play defense. He has to want to do it. To me, defense is hard work, determination and desire.

When I play defense, I try to play as big as I can. That is, I want to take up as much room as I can take up, to present the biggest obstacle I possibly can. Therefore, I stand up straight and spread my arms out as far as possible. I stand in a position in which I can move quickly and, of course, I stay alert.

Just as I do on offense, I try to vary my position and my moves on defense so as not to fall into any predictable pattern. I try to change the angle on my man, meaning I do not position myself always between him and the basket in the same angle. Sometimes I try to "front" a man, especially one who is taller than I am; but when I do that I am exposing one side of the basket and I must have help from a teammate on that weak side.

There are times when I might be forced into a situation where the opposition has a two-on-one and I'm the one. If that happens, if I'm split by two men, I try to show myself

This is what we call "fronting" a man. *(Farrell)*

to the man outside, make him conscious of my presence with the hope of distracting him or getting him to hesitate just a little. Then I slide back to the man inside because he presents a more serious threat to score. If I delay the outside man long enough, maybe one of my teammates can get through to pick him up and I'm free to cover the man underneath.

Every ballplayer develops a style or pattern of basketball play and generally he's going to follow that style or pattern 90 per cent of the time. So you know before the game starts that this is the kind of shot Wilt's going to use and these are the kinds of shots Alcindor will take or Wes Unseld or Elvin Hayes. You know pretty much what they like to do because you play against them so often. But that's not saying you're going to be able to stop them.

My conception of defense is that I want to try to get my opponent to do things he does not ordinarily do. I want to force him into taking shots that are not his best shots. I want to exploit his weakness. If I can take away his strength and force him to go to his weakness, that's in my favor.

Every player has a favorite shot or a favorite position on a particular shot. My job is to keep him from taking that favorite shot or to deny him that position. I know I'm not going to be able to stop him from taking his shot all the time, but if I can get him to take that shot 2 or 3 feet farther out than he normally shoots it, that's going to cut down on his accuracy.

People have asked me who is the easiest center in the NBA for me to play against. My answer to that is I haven't found him yet. Sure, there are some who are tougher than others, but there are no bad centers in the NBA. Every one of them makes you work for your living. Any guy in there can hurt you or he wouldn't be there. All of them are tough. There's no night when you can say, "Oh, I've got Joe Jones tonight, it's going to be an easy night." They've all got ability, they've all got their strengths and they come out to play. They come out to beat you every night.

I would have to say that the toughest offensively are Wilt

Wilt Chamberlain shoots his famous scoop shot. *(United Press International Photo)*

Chamberlain, Lew Alcindor and Elvin Hayes. And the toughest on defense are Nate Thurmond and Wes Unseld.

I'll give you a rundown of the centers I have to play against and what I have to look for against each of them.

WILT CHAMBERLAIN. The first time I ever played against Wilt was in San Francisco. I scored 28 points and I thought I did a helluva job on him—until I looked at the statistics sheet. He had 54 points. That's the kind of player Chamberlain is. He has so much ability, you think you're stopping him, but when you look up he's got his 30 or 40 points.

When Wilt gets close to the basket, he's almost impossible to stop. He's got a good scoop shot and he's just so strong. If there's a missed shot and he's in close to the hoop, he'll go right over you to get the rebound. Like everybody else, Chamberlain has his strengths and his weaknesses, although his strengths far outnumber his weaknesses. When he goes to his left, I know 90 per cent of the time what shot he's going to take—and 99 per cent of the time I know I'm not going to stop the shot. All I can do is make him know I'm there, get my body right in his way if I can and force him to knock me over before I'll give him that easy shot in close.

On the right side, he'll use that fallaway jumper of his— also an impossible shot to stop. There, I try to get him to take the shot farther out than he'd like to take it.

Wilt's liabilities are really physical ones; his knee injury, for instance. After he came back from the injury, he didn't have the mobility he once had.

The basic thing I have to do against Chamberlain is to try to beat him with quickness. I can't go inside and contest him because he's just too big. Any guy 7 feet tall, I'd have trouble contesting inside, so I have to assume I'm going to be quicker than he is.

There's not much you can do against Chamberlain on defense, so I just play sound, basic, logical defense.

LEW ALCINDOR. Lew presents just about the same problems as Chamberlain because of his height. I believe he's 7 feet, 3 inches, at least. I know for a fact that he's taller than Chamberlain, and Wilt is 7–2. I try to keep Lew from going in close to the basket because that's where he likes to operate. He has great moves in there, unbelievable moves for someone who has been playing so short a time.

There's just no way you're going to stop a guy as tall as Alcindor once he gets in close to the basket unless you're taller than he is, or as tall. Alcindor is very tough when he comes down and sits out there on the left side of the court. In fact, he's very tough when he comes down and sits out there on the right side.

A lot of people said he wouldn't make it in the NBA because he's slim and looks frail. They said he wasn't strong enough, that he wouldn't be able to take the physical abuse you have to take as a center in the NBA. I never believed those stories. I figured any player as tall and as agile as he is had to make it. Bill Russell wasn't physical and he made it for thirteen years in the league. In the long run, I'm sorry to say, Lew proved I was right.

The thing about Lew, too, is that you know he's going to get better each year as he gets more experience. Do I worry about him getting better? Why should I worry about something I can't control?

During the summer after we won the championship, people kept asking me if I was worried about Milwaukee because the club got Oscar Robertson to go with Alcindor. My answer was: "Why should I start worrying about Alcindor now when I don't have to go out and play him until October? Let me at least enjoy my summer." That's my philosophy about the game of basketball. I stop worrying about it as soon as the season ends. Summer is for relaxing, for hunting and fishing, which are my two main hobbies. There's plenty of time to worry about basketball when the season starts again in October.

WES UNSELD. When I think of Unseld, I think of the word "unselfish." His name even sounds like "unselfish." That's my impression of Wes, a completely unselfish player, the

Although noted for defense, Nate Thurmond can hurt you with his jumper. *(Malcolm W. Emmons)*

most unselfish player on his team. He's a great player. He'll do whatever has to be done to help his team win; if it means that he won't shoot once all night, if it means trying to get every rebound that comes off the boards, he'll do it or die trying.

He could be a better offensive center if he set out to do so. After all, he averaged 26 points a game in college, so you know he can shoot. It's just that there are so many good offensive players around him, somebody's got to do the rebounding. Rebounding is his job on the team, so he sacrifices himself for the good of the team. That's the kind of team player you like to have.

He tries to get most of his points on the offensive board, off tips and rebounds or easy layups when he's underneath. You'll notice that the Bullets became a contending team when they got Wes. That's his value to his team. He's not very tall for a center, only 6–7, but he's broad and strong.

On offense, I try to use my height advantage on him. He's one of the few centers in the NBA I have a height advantage against. On defense, you've got to pound away with him because he's rugged. And I've got the bumps and bruises to prove it.

NATE THURMOND. He's tough around the basket, too, because of his height. He goes to the offensive board really well and he's got a good jumper and a good hook. His turnaround jumper is good too. He can fool you with it. A lot of times you say to yourself he's not going to make that shot, but he does.

However, the real threat of Nate is his defense. He's the toughest in the league defensively. He's fast, he's massive and he covers a large area in there with his long arms and quick reflexes. You really have to be thinking when you play him. You never take a thing for granted against Nate because he'll go wherever you go and he'll come out of nowhere to block your shot.

ELVIN HAYES. He's the best shooter among the centers in the league. He's got a quick release on his shot and he can

I consider Elvin Hayes the best shooting center in the NBA. *(Malcolm W. Emmons)*

hit from anywhere. He'll take you outside, and you have to be ready to go with him because you can't give him too much room. If you do, it's 2 points. The fact that he goes outside so much presents a lot of problems in rebounding. When he goes out, I have to go with him, and somebody else, DeBusschere or Bradley, has to be ready to grab the rebound. That's why the philosophy of team defense is so important.

BOB RULE. I remember the first game of the season during our championship year against the Seattle SuperSonics. Rule just did everything. He scored 17 points in the first half, and Dick Barnett said he thought he was going to have to call out the fire department, hot as Rule was. I've always had trouble with Rule. He runs well and he's very tough around the basket. I find him tough to play because he's left-handed. Maybe that sounds strange because I'm also left-handed, but remember, there aren't many centers in pro ball who are left-handed and I'm not used to playing *against* a southpaw. He's shooting into my weak hand all the time. So I have to assume if he's trouble for me because he's left-handed, I must be trouble for him.

WALT BELLAMY. For my money, my old teammate is the best driving center in the league. He'll surprise you with his speed—he can really take off in there; he can really get to the basket. That means that if he gets the ball, he's going to cause some damage, so you try to keep him from getting the ball in a position where he can drive on you.

DARRALL IMHOFF. Darrall is a good, solid center, the kind of ballplayer who plays every night and won't hurt his team even if he won't be spectacular. He'll get his 12 rebounds a game and his 12 or 14 points a game. He's steady and solid and he doesn't make many mistakes on defense. He's been around a while and knows how to play the game. On offense, he handles the ball very well. I have a lot of respect for Darrall as a center who knows his job and does it well.

TOM BOERWINKLE. He's a very improved center. And he keeps getting better. He shoots a good hook shot and does a good job rebounding and setting picks. His size presents a problem. He's massive: 7 feet and close to 275 pounds. Sometimes when I play him I can't even be seen behind him.

OTTO MOORE and BOB LANIER. I have to couple these two because the way the Pistons play, they platoon their centers. Otto and Bob each play about half the game and each has his own role with the team as well as his particular strengths. They complement each other very well. Moore is the defensive specialist, Lanier the offensive center. Otto is excellent on defense. He's agile and quick and has good reactions. He jumps exceptionally well and he's a good rebounder. His shooting needs improvement, but that will come with experience and practice.

I remember Lanier from the summer he spent at my basketball camp between his junior and senior years in college. I knew then he was going to be a good pro. He's a great offensive player. He's another left-hander and has a great shooting touch. He can go outside and hit and he's unbelievably fast for a man his size. In college he had a weight problem, but running up and down in the NBA took care of that. His problem as a rookie was that he had just undergone a knee operation. His knee still wasn't at full strength and that hurt his mobility. Let me tell you, I'm an expert on trying to play pro basketball with a knee problem.

DAVE COWENS. Dave surprised a lot of people by the way he came into the NBA and did such a tremendous job as a center. He had been expected to play forward, but the Celtics needed him in the hole. Like me, he's a left-handed shooter, and it seems that most left-handed centers are good shooters. Dave is not only a very good shooter; he's an active center and runs a lot. In that respect, he's a lot like me. I'm an active center and I think Dave benefited from playing forward, as I did.

HENRY FINKEL. While Cowens is resting or if the Celtics need more height, they bring in Henry Finkel. He's a bit slow, but he's a very good shooter—another left-hander. He has a good hook shot and he presents two problems: one because he's left-handed, the other because he's a 7-footer.

NEAL WALK and JIM FOX. In his rookie year, Neal Walk shared the position with Jim Fox, so I didn't get to see too much of Walk. My impression when I did see him was that he went to the boards well, but I wasn't too sure about his shooting. I thought Jimmy was a better shooter, although Walk was strong and better defensively and I felt he would improve. I was right. The Suns traded Fox, and it was up to Walk to do the job. Getting the job probably helped his confidence, and he got better because he was playing more often. His shooting improved tremendously and he became a very good center, big, strong and tough defensively.

BOB KAUFFMAN. The greatest thing that ever happened to him was expansion. He got a chance to play regularly and he made the All-Star team, which proves that a lot of guys could be outstanding players if they got the chance. There's a lot of talent in this league that hasn't been tapped. Kauffman is a good center. He runs well, he rebounds well and he has a good outside shot. In reality, he's not a center. He plays more like a forward, which could be a factor in his success. He's always moving, which is not what a true center does, and that makes him difficult to defend against.

LE ROY ELLIS. Le Roy has been around a long time, but he's played better for Portland than he ever did. I think he got better as he got older. Of course, here again, he has had a better opportunity to play than ever before. He's a good shooter and a good rebounder and he runs unusually well. He's slender and though he appears to lack strength, he's strong—believe me. He knows the league and that helps too.

WALT WESLEY. He is finally getting a chance to play a lot, but hasn't been able to develop consistently. Some nights he has a great shot; some nights he can't seem to make a basket. He plays good defense and I think all he needs is experience. It will be just a matter of time before he becomes one of the top centers in the league. Of course, he's very slim and he lacks strength and stamina and that could hold him back.

For my money, Walt Bellamy (31) is the best driving center in the league. *(United Press International Photo)*

The best way to get into shape is to run, run, run. *(United Press International Photo)*

10

Shaping Up

You have to have height to play center in the National Basketball Association. But you also have to have strength and stamina.

Height is a gift of nature. Strength and stamina can be acquired. But there is no easy way. They are acquired with hard work.

As a boy, Willis Reed worked hard, picking cotton and working in flower beds. When he got a little older, he hauled hay. All of these things contributed to developing a body strong enough to battle the monsters who play center in the NBA.

But the work didn't stop there. In many ways it gets tougher: there is preseason training and, the constant, daily discipline of getting sufficient rest, and once the season has begun, eating the proper foods.

Conditioning can be the making of a professional athlete. It can also be his undoing.

I think that when you're young and growing quickly and you begin to get interested in sports, one of the most important things is your diet. You're outside playing ball all day, burning up all that energy, and you've got to have the right foods to supply you with all the energy you need.

It's important that you eat the proper foods—meat and green vegetables—and drink plenty of milk. If you eat all the foods your body needs for growing purposes, you'll be all right.

One problem with most youngsters is that even though their mothers prepare the right foods, they won't eat them because they don't like them. But certain foods must be eaten because they give youngsters the basic requirements for growing.

Occasionally, especially when we're on the road and flying all around the country, eating at irregular hours and sometimes eating on the run, I fail to eat the proper foods myself. What I do to make sure I get all the basic requirements is take vitamins. I used to take vitamin pills, but I've had trouble with my stomach and, for some reason, they just won't go down in the morning when I'm supposed to take them. Instead, the doctor gives me a vitamin shot about once a week.

But I recommend vitamin pills for youngsters, not as a replacement for the foods they should be eating, but as a supplement. Any one-a-day vitamin that you buy in the drugstore is good and should be taken at mealtime, preferably in the morning.

Some of the players in the NBA are practically fanatic about conditioning, and that's good. Cazzie Russell drinks carrot juice and eats wheat germ. I can't do any of that stuff. I just don't like it. A lot of players eat a candy bar or take some honey before the game for quick energy, but I don't do that either. I just can't eat anything right before a game.

What I do is take dextrose tablets, which is sugar, and that gives me quick energy. I may take some vitamin C tablets if I'm feeling a little run-down and I take salt tablets to replace the salt in my body that I will lose from perspiring so much.

A lot of youngsters have asked me how I feel about lifting weights. Generally speaking, I think it's all right under the proper supervision. Like anything else, it can be overdone. I think it all depends on how big a boy we're talking about. If you mean a big boy who's going to get bigger, he's going to have to do a lot of things, like lifting weights and jumping rope to help his coordination. These are things the smaller boy may not have to do, but the bigger boy will find that his coordination will not be right because he's growing so rapidly. So he needs these things to develop his body and his agility.

I didn't lift weights in high school, but I did a lot of hard work which served the same purpose: it helped develop my body. Some of that, though, is hereditary.

I work with weights now, but I don't overdo it. I lift about 60 pounds, which is not a lot for someone my size. I'm looking for muscle tone and a little strength in my shoulders and arms. I put the weights over my shoulders and do deep knee bends, which are good for my knees. I go down to the point where I have the most stress; then I raise up on the balls of my feet.

These things are not going to hurt me. It's not as if I'm lifting 150 or 200 pounds. Even in college I lifted 60 pounds, just enough to achieve my objective of tone and strength.

A lot of youngsters have taken to using weights on their ankles when they play. They think it will help them become better rebounders on the theory that when they remove the weights, their legs will feel lighter and they will be able to jump higher.

I question that theory, but that's not my main objection. I just think it's something that is definitely dangerous. To walk around with weights on your shoes is all right, but to play with them can be harmful. I think a lot of youngsters have developed knee problems from playing with weights.

One thing that is definitely harmful, especially for basketball players, is smoking. It cuts your wind, and basketball is a game in which wind is very important because you're running all the time. Smoking is just a bad habit. I think most youngsters start out smoking because it makes them feel grown up. Then, once they've started, it's a very difficult habit to break and it could affect their playing.

There has been a lot of talk lately about professional athletes taking pills, stimulants, drugs that pep them up. I don't know what others do, but I know that I have never taken these kinds of drugs and I never will.

I put the use of such drugs in the same class with smoking, drinking and staying out late at night. They all come under the heading of abusing your body. In an earlier chapter I discussed the danger of abusing the body. I think it bears repeating here. My basic philosophy is that my body is my greatest asset in my business—the business of playing basketball—and I'm not going to be foolish enough to do anything that might destroy that asset.

Another important thing for the young ballplayer is that he get proper rest. That goes along with eating the right foods. If you don't get enough rest, you won't be able to do the job the way you're supposed to.

When I was young, I used to have to be home by nine-thirty at night and I'd be in bed before ten. And I would get up at seven in the morning, which gave me nine hours' sleep.

Even now I try to get as much rest as I can. When we're on the road, I usually get up around eleven if we've played a game the night before or if we've been traveling and get to the hotel late. After I have my breakfast, I go back to my room. Usually I can't sleep, so I just lie down and rest.

I try to have my pregame meal sometime between two and three in the afternoon, usually a steak. I can't eat any later than that on the day of a game. I wish I could. I think it would give me a little more energy for the second half of the game, which is often the most important part. I've tried to eat closer to game time, say at five o'clock for a seven-thirty game, but I just can't do it. It won't go down. You can put the best piece of steak in the world in front of me and, as much as I love steak, it won't go down.

By that time the adrenalin is beginning to flow in my body

and that's why I can't eat. I'm beginning to get hypoed by that time. It's not a conscious thing, your system begins to hypo by itself.

After my pregame meal, I go back up to my room to lie down and rest again. Sometimes I can sleep before a game; sometimes I can't. It all depends on the situation and the importance of the game. Even if I don't fall asleep, at least I'm resting.

When it's time to leave for the arena, I get up and, whether I have slept or not, I take a shower. It helps refresh me and wake me up.

Now I'm ready to go to work.

One of the subjects I cover at my summer camp is how to prepare for a game. *(Farrell)*

11
"Not Much Chance to Get Weary"

Willis Reed goes to work in smoke-filled arenas, some with better lighting than others, some bigger than others, some with more spectators than others.

If he has just flown from East Coast to West Coast and lost three hours, the clock will say eight o'clock, but his body will say eleven o'clock when he goes to work.

He may be playing his third game in three consecutive nights or he may be playing his first game in a week. He may be in his groove or he may be in a slump.

The fans may be for him or cheering their mightiest against him. It could be a meaningless game in November or it could be the game to determine the champion of the National Basketball Association.

He could be playing in Detroit in the dead of winter with the outside temperatures below zero or he could be playing in balmy Los Angeles with the temperature outside reaching into the eighties.

In all cases, Willis Reed must be prepared. He must be ready for anything and everything when the buzzer rings, signaling the start of the game. After that, it's too late.

139

When I walk onto a floor twenty minutes before a ball game, I have to get the feel of that court. I have to get the feel of the rim, the feel of the environment, get adjusted to the lighting. I walk around and look around to make sure I have familiarized myself with everything, every bit of the surroundings—the floor, the stands, the shadows, everything.

We play sixteen different teams in sixteen different arenas, not including Madison Square Garden, and the way the schedule is set up, it may be a month or two between visits to a particular arena. So it is necessary to reacquaint myself with the surroundings.

In addition to getting my eyes reaccustomed to the lighting, I try to find out if the basket is a hard-shooting basket or a soft-shooting one; if the rebound is going to bounce long or short off the rim after a missed shot; if it's high or low on one side or in the front. If the shots are not dropping during practice, I have to find out why and make the necessary adjustment and I have only a short time to do it.

I don't believe in wearing myself out in practice. I'd rather save my stamina for the game. In this league, there is so much traveling, which tires you, that I try to maintain my sharpness for the game with a minimum amount of effort.

Sometimes things that apply to me or any other professional basketball player do not apply to the younger fellows in high school or college. That includes warming up before a game. The youngster growing up should practice as much as he can and shoot as many shots as he can because he's in a developmental stage. At the stage of the game I am in right now, where we are playing almost every night, there is not as much time to practice as there is in a high school or college schedule.

I try not to have to go out and shoot a lot of shots before a game. I don't feel I have to shoot a hundred shots to get ready. A lot of players will come to the arena, dress and shoot an hour before the game, then come back in to the dressing room and go out again twenty minutes before the game when the whole team warms up. Maybe it's a mental thing, but I tend to have bad ball games when I do that.

To play my position and to produce, I need to conserve my energy as much as I can. Not that the shooting is going to bother me, but the idea is to try to get ready to play at maximum potential without having to overpractice to do so. I like to be able to go out and be ready to play a game after taking twenty jump shots, thirty or forty shots altogether.

I figure I have only those twenty minutes before the game to get ready and instead of using all that time for shooting, I'm using it to get my legs loose, my timing down and myself generally situated in the arena.

There are only so many shots I can take in the time I allow myself for shooting before a game. So, first, I take all the shots I figure to use in the game that night. That's determined by who my opponent is that night (maybe I have better success with one shot or another against certain opponents) or by what shot has been working for me in recent games. The rest of the time I use to try all the shots I possess, about five or six of each. Then I'll give extra attention— about ten or twelve shots—to the one I feel needs the most work.

Crowds vary with different cities. In some of the newer cities in the league, the crowds are rather quiet, cheering only when their team does something good. In some of the older cities in the league, the crowds are much more vocal. I try to put the crowd noise out of my mind. In Philadelphia, for instance, the fans are especially tough on the players, but I do my best not to hear what they say. If you're concentrating on your job, you won't hear what the fans are saying. Sure, you hear the crowd noise, but it's more like a steady hum. You're not picking up individual voices and comments.

The players who go to the gym and shoot for an hour the afternoon of a game are usually the players who do not play regularly and want to stay sharp. I rarely do that. The only exception is when I feel there's something wrong with my shot. Then I figure I need to go out and get some extra work on it to get it ready. Usually, however, I figure resting is more important than practicing. With two or three games every week and practice almost every day when there is no game, there is not much chance to get weary.

Another thing I avoid is any kind of calisthenics or warm-ups before a game. A great one for that is Cazzie Russell, but I just don't have that kind of energy.

I had Cazzie as a guest lecturer at my basketball camp and one boy asked him what he does to get ready. Cazzie went through his entire routine, the isometrics, the calisthenics, the jumping drills, the running in place, the push-ups, the sit-ups.

Later that same day Dick Barnett was a guest lecturer. The same boy had a question for Dick.

"Cazzie Russell told us everything he does in the dressing room before a game to get ready. What do you do?"

"I just watch Cazzie going through his routine," Dick said, "and after looking at him, I'm ready to play."

That's exactly the way I feel. Sometimes I don't know where Cazzie gets his energy. You can get tired just watching him.

During the game Red Holzman has a routine worked out for me. I usually play the whole twelve minutes of the first period. Then I play the first eight minutes of the second period and take a blow. If I'm needed, I come back after about a two-minute rest. If not, I won't play again until the start of the second half. Then I play the entire second half depending on how the game is going. If we've got one of those rare runaways ("laughers," the players call them), Red gives me a rest.

If the pace is particularly hectic and I have to take a blow during a game, I take it when we're on offense because that's when you don't look bad and you can't hurt the team too badly. With the kind of ballplayers we have on the Knicks, there's always someone to take up the slack on the offensive end. But defensively, I have to always do my job because if DeBusschere, Bradley, Barnett and Frazier, any of the guys, are playing their game and doing what they're supposed to be doing—dropping off their man, helping out, double-teaming the man with the ball, all the things that comprise the well-integrated team defense we play—there are going to be situations when they will need my help on defense. If there's going to be a mental lapse on the floor, it's best that it comes on the offensive end.

There's no pattern to what it's like in the Knick dressing room before a game. It varies. Sometimes the guys are very loose, laughing and joking, and sometimes they are very serious. It depends on the situation, the team we're playing, the importance of the game, whether we've been on a long road trip, if we've played a lot of games in recent days, whether we're rested or tired. All these things influence the pregame mood.

Every game on every night in every town is a different situation, and the thing I did last night, I might not do to-night. It's true that players fall into a playing pattern just as people fall into a pattern of behavior, but playing basketball is not like putting your shoe on and tying it the same way every day. Every situation is different.

There are certain teams that we know we don't have much trouble with, that we've done well against. On nights when we play those teams, there is not much pressure on us and the atmosphere in the dressing room is relaxed.

Then there are teams that we have not done so well with and when we're playing against them the dressing room scene is much more serious.

There is no such thing as one team "psyching" another in professional sports. You hear that term tossed around a lot, but I believe it's a lot of nonsense. It implies that one team is afraid of another or intimidated by another, but you just don't frighten professionals.

As often as we play, it's hard to predict what kind of game we're going to have, judging from what the atmosphere in the dressing room is like. The one thing I like to see is for us to have a good warm-up. If we warm up and the ball is dropping and the guys are chattering and loose, I figure we're going to play well. Whether we're going to win or not, I don't know, but I figure we'll play well and it won't be one of those games when we're blown off the court and embarrassed. Luckily, we haven't had many of those recently.

What I do after the game usually depends on the kind of game it was. Maybe I'll go for a sandwich or maybe I won't feel like eating. If it was an easy game and we won, I go get something to eat. If we've lost or it was a close, tense game, I won't be able to eat.

Despite what you may have read, athletes don't go doing a lot of running around on the road. I know I don't. In fact, I get more rest on the road than I do at home, when there always seems to be something to do, some errand to run. On the road, I rarely leave the hotel, not even to eat. In my rookie year, I did a little sight-seeing—the usual things like Fishermen's Wharf and the street cars in San Francisco, Disneyland in Los Angeles, the San Diego Zoo. But I've cut out that sight-seeing. It's too tiring. I figure I can do all the sight-seeing I want when I'm through playing basketball. Right now, basketball is my job. I might have to go out and play Wilt Chamberlain and I know that's going to take all the energy I have. I'm not being fair to my teammates if I'm out sight-seeing the day I have to play against Chamberlain.

The same is true with friends. I have friends all over the country, people I went to school with or people I've met through the years. They come up to see me after a game and they say, "Hey, man, let's go out." Or they invite me to their house for dinner.

Most of the time I have to say no. Or say, "Okay, we'll go out for a quick bite to eat, but I have to be back at the hotel by twelve."

Sometimes I offend them, but I can't help it. They come to the game to relax. I'm there to work. Basketball is my job and my job has to come first—even before my friends.

When we lose a game and we can say that the other team really beat us, that's not so bad. That kind of loss we can take.

But if we lost a close game and we beat ourselves or if I made a mistake and we actually gave the game away, that kind of game really gets to me. Some nights we're going to get beat and all we can say is we got run off the court and there wasn't much we could do about it.

Sometimes you can rationalize a defeat. Maybe we've played three nights in a row or we just came off a long trip and we're tired. We gave it a good effort, but we lost. You can forget that kind. It's the ones that you should have won and didn't that hurt. After those games I have trouble sleeping.

As soon as I can, I begin thinking about the next game. That's not easy to do after a tough defeat, but after a game is lost, it's lost, and there's nothing you can do about it except look ahead.

If I have a game tonight and one tomorrow night and, hopefully, we've won this game tonight, I think about the parts of my game that are going well. I'll go back and re-evaluate my whole game. Is my jump shot effective? Am I driving well? Am I rebounding? Do I feel springy under the boards? I'm re-evaluating my performance with reference to what I did to help the team or where I might need some polishing up. That will help me decide what to work on in pregame practice tomorrow or which shots to concentrate on in the game.

After that, unless we're playing the same team the following night, I think about the team we're playing next. In particular, I'm thinking about the center I'll be coming up against. What are his strengths? What are his weaknesses? I'll run them over in my mind.

Then I'll check the newspapers. If that team has played the night before, I'll check the box scores to see how my opponent did. That gives me some insight into what frame of mind he may be in. If he's been scoring well, I know I've got to go out and play him tough right from the beginning, to try to discourage him and not let him get off to a good start.

As soon as one game is over, I start preparing for the next game, even if it's four or five days away. If I have that much time, I start preparing in a casual way. It's not like cramming for an exam or anything. All the days that I'm not playing and my opponent is playing, I check the papers to see how he's doing. All the while, I get flashbacks of things I might have done to blow a ball game or something I did that was good and that I had better try again in the next game.

I don't rely on what I read in the newspapers, except what I see in the box scores. I read the newspapers all the time, even after a bad night, because, let's face it, you can't escape from reality. If I played badly and the writer says I played badly, why should I be upset at him?

If someone writes an uncomplimentary article about me, it all depends on who the writer is. If I know the writer and I think he's competent enough to know what he's talking about and if he's telling the truth, I can't get mad at him. That man has to make his living too. Newspapers are necessary in the world of professional sports and so are sportswriters. Through the years, I've found most of them to be fair, but there are exceptions.

During the championship playoff against the Lakers, I read in the papers that Chamberlain was going to play a certain distance from the basket. Well, I know from playing Wilt that he's only going to go just so far from the basket; I don't need a newspaper to tell me. These are just common facts. A newspaperman can't tell me something about a guy I have to play against except that he's hurt, and even then I don't believe it. If I go out there and the whistle blows and he's not in uniform, that's when I believe it.

What it comes down to is depending more on myself and my judgment. With reference to the players I have to play against, my judgment is better than any newspaperman's.

As I said, I have been very fortunate in that I have always gotten a good press. But then I contribute, too, by always trying to cooperate. It's not that I'm looking for them to say nice things about me; it's just that I know the man has a job to do just as I have a job to do. He earns his bread and butter for his family by writing about me and I earn my bread and butter by playing basketball.

I've always said that all I ever want anybody to say about me when I'm through playing basketball is: "Willis Reed gave 100 per cent all the time."

Our worst break: Cazzie's ankle. *(United Press International Photo)*

12

A Team at Last

Dave DeBusschere became a Knick midway in the 1969–70 season and within weeks it was as if he had always been a Knick. He blended perfectly as an integral part of Red Holzman's offense and defense and as a member of the cast.

DeBusschere was the perfect complement for Willis Reed on the court. He helped Reed fight the mastodons of the NBA for rebounds, and they helped each other on defense. They also found a common bond of interests and beliefs off the court and they became close friends.

As the 1970–71 season drew to a close, they planned a hunting trip in Wyoming in the off-season. "We'll hunt antelope, elk and bear," said Reed. "That is, if there's anything left to hunt the way things are going in this country."

The arrival of DeBusschere had been the missing piece in the puzzle, the finishing touch to a great masterwork of art.

On December 27, 1967, Red Holzman replaced Dick McGuire as coach, with the Knicks in the last place with a record of 15–22. They won twenty-eight of the next forty-five games, finished in third place and made the playoffs for only the third time in thirteen years.

149

Then came December 19, 1969, and Dave DeBusschere became a Knick. Suddenly, everything had fallen neatly in place.

Now we were a team, a unit, a group of men putting out that unified effort that Red Holzman likes to talk about. It wasn't just one man or one thing that made us good. It was a multitude of things falling into place at the same time. In a way, we were like a well-oiled, smooth-functioning machine, with every gear doing its job.

There was Walt Frazier running the ball club; Dave DeBusschere playing the tough defense and doing a huge share of the rebounding; Bill Bradley, the man for whom we called set plays; Dick Barnett, the tough defensive guard and the hot shooter who could break a game apart suddenly; Cazzie Russell coming off the bench to give us a lift; Nate Bowman, the guy who came in to give me a blow. Everybody had a job and everybody did his job.

There was a closeness on the Knicks, a kind of special ESP on the court. Each man knew the other man's moves, his strengths, what his job was. We were playing together as a team with a kind of sixth sense that told us where to pass, when to pass and to whom we should pass. It's difficult to explain how we knew, but we knew. And everything began to click. We were winning, and the more we won, the more confident we became. We got the feeling that we could go out on the court and beat any team in the league.

There was a lot of publicity at the time about the amount of money the Knicks had to pay to get Bradley and Russell to sign, and a lot of people naturally thought there was some resentment among a few of us older fellows who have been around longer and never got that kind of money. I think the feeling of the fellows on the team was that it was just a matter of situations and timing. We were logical and realistic enough to realize that the timing was right for Cazzie and Bill. We understood that and we certainly had no re-

Players like Oscar Robertson come along once in a lifetime. *(Malcolm W. Emmons)*

sentment toward them for getting whatever they could.

Everybody on the Knicks knows that if he does his job, he's going to be well compensated. I don't know of any of my teammates who have any complaints in that respect.

When Bradley and Russell signed, there was some talk that each was going to be another Oscar Robertson. Personally, I never believed it. I never thought they had that kind of talent. That's not taking anything away from Cazzie and Bill because, after all, an Oscar Robertson comes along just once in a lifetime. Bradley and Russell are both fantastic basketball players. They don't need to be compared to anybody else.

If people want to know how good Bill Bradley is, all they have to do is realize that the man is a star on a team of stars.

I say the Knicks are a team of stars. They are also a team without a superstar. And I don't think any man on our team is worried about becoming a superstar. There are no prima donnas on the Knickerbockers. Every player is concerned only with winning. I mean, would you rather be a superstar on a losing team or a star on a winning team?

Of all the things that are important, I think to be on a winning team, to be part of a winner, is the most important thing for a professional athlete. Look at Elgin Baylor and Jerry West, for instance. They are two of the greatest players who ever played the game. They've done everything you can do in basketball; they've both won just about every honor a man can win. But they've never played on a winner. Knowing them, I'm sure both would trade all those honors if they could play on a championship team—just once.

Being on a winning team is more important than anything else. It's more than being the league's leading scorer or the league's Most Valuable Player or anything.

I think I'm a winner. I play to win and everything I do, I do with the idea of winning. I played on a lot of losing teams from the time I was in high school, but I always knew that one day I would be on a winner. If you give 100 per cent plus, it's only a matter of time before you win.

I had to wait six years in the NBA before I played on a

winner. I don't think six years is too long to wait to be on a championship team. I have the satisfaction of knowing that for one year we were the best in the world.

I said before that the Knicks are a very close team. I mean we are close on the court, in our thinking, in the way we play the game. We're not particularly close off the court. Most of the guys go pretty much their own way. But I don't think it's important for us to be close off the court for us to win. Professional athletes don't have to be close.

We see enough of each other. We travel together, we're on planes together, on buses together, in the locker room before and after the game together, we play in games together. There's only so much you want to see of guys you play ball with.

I spend more time with my teammates than most people spend with their families. We're together more during the season than people who work in the same office from nine to five. I'm not interested in going out with Frazier or Barnett on the road. I have other interests and other friends whom I don't see that much of and I'd like to be with them when I go on the road.

In fact, I think it's good for a team if the players do not get too close to one another. The one thing each member of the Knicks has is respect for each man as a man, and that's the most important thing. The guys are unselfish; they're willing to sacrifice for the good of the team. Players on our team give up good shots and pass to another player because he might have a better shot.

Passing is one of the greatest assets of the Knicks. You don't see one man dribble down and take the shot. We average three passes before the shot. And we never force our shots. There's one basic rule that all youngsters should learn: *You can pass a ball faster than you can dribble it.*

When you've got that kind of concept going, you've got a winning attitude. That's more important than going out with your teammates.

When I first joined the Knicks, my roommate was Emmette Bryant and we became close friends. After Emmette left and I was made captain of the team, I began rooming with rookies. First it was Bill Hosket, then John Warren, then Mike Price.

It's no particular advantage rooming with a rookie. I mean, they don't bring me breakfast in bed or carry my bag or anything like that.

They didn't room me with rookies because I couldn't get along with the other players on the team. I get along with all of them. I can room with any of them. I think the idea of rooming me with a rookie came from our trainer, Danny Whelan. He figured it would be good for the rookie breaking in to room with me because I am the captain of the team and maybe I can help him in some little way.

Danny is always thinking of things like that. He's a man who has never scored a point or grabbed a rebound for the Knicks, yet he has had a lot to do with our success. He's tremendous for team morale. He walks around with a long cigar in his mouth and his hands jammed in his pockets, and the guys on the team call him "Big-time Danny Whelan."

Danny spent most of his time in baseball. He was the trainer for the Pittsburgh Pirates when they won the World Series in 1960 and he's always talking about his days with the Pirates. I think Danny's first love is baseball, but I also think we're winning him over to basketball. He's always in a happy frame of mind, laughing and telling stories. Some of them are even true. When the guys are down, he picks them up. He may be taping somebody's ankle and if there's a lot of tension in the room because it's a big game coming up, Danny will start his routine.

"I can tell I'm taping a winner," he will say. "Yep, I can feel it. I'm taping a winner."

And the next thing we know, he'll have us laughing and joking and very loose. I think he's great for the team, not only as a trainer, but as a morale builder.

After DeBusschere arrived, we really started playing ball. One of our greatest assets on the Knicks is our consistency in scoring. We have good balanced scoring from our forwards, guards and center, and also from our bench.

We developed some set plays and worked on them until we had perfected them and they proved to be very effective for us. One of our favorite plays is the "back door play," which Bradley and Frazier work to perfection. It ends up with Frazier scoring a layup. It has been one of our most effective plays, and its success depends entirely on teamwork.

An example of what I mean by the way we play together and think together is that Bradley and DeBusschere have developed a style where they play wide of the basket. That helps me because I like to have room to work in the hole. And I won't go out in their territory and bring my man out to interfere with them. I will rarely take a shot from the corner. There are several reasons. There is no backboard to use as a guide, and I'm too far away to follow up my shot. But the most important reason is if I miss, I'm too far out of position to get back on defense. I'd be the last man down court. Dick Barnett can shoot from the corners and get away with it for one very good reason—he makes most of those shots.

All of the Knicks have one common thought: you've got to play to beat everybody every night. If you play a team six times during the season and you're pretty evenly matched, there are going to be two times when you're at your best and maybe two times when the other team is at its best. Let's say you split those four games. It's those remaining two games that are up for grabs, and the team with more determination and hustle is going to win them. And that will be the difference between a championship team and an also-ran.

It used to be that year after year you'd go against a team and know what to expect. The personality of a team is reflected by the coach, but in recent years there have been so many coaching changes that the personalities of teams have also changed.

Los Angeles, for example, played a high post (the center out near the keyhole) when Bill Van Breda Kolff was coach, but under Joe Mullaney they were a low-post (the center in deep under the basket) team.

Here I demonstrate how to give off to a guard cutting off the center. *(Farrell)*

Here I pick off the defensive guard to enable the offensive guard (in white) to go for an uncontested layup. *(Farrell)*

About the only team that didn't change for a long time was the Boston Celtics because of Red Auerbach and Bill Russell. When you went out to play the Celtics, you always knew they were going to be extremely tough and aggressive on defense and they were going to play a run-and-shoot game on offense.

We were coming on and for the last half of the 1968–69 season, we played the best ball in the NBA. We came close, but we couldn't catch the Baltimore Bullets, who had built up a huge early lead and held on to finish first in the Eastern Division. We finished third, one game behind Philadelphia and two games behind Baltimore, which meant we had to play the Bullets in the playoffs.

We were happy with the match-up. We thought we were a better ball club and here was our chance to prove it. I don't think anybody expected what happened in the playoffs. We beat the Bullets in four straight games and faced the Boston Celtics for the Eastern Division championship.

The Celtics had finished six games behind us in the regular season, and a lot of people figured they were over the hill. Truthfully, we didn't. Especially when they beat the 76ers, four games to one, in their playoff. We knew the Celtics would be tough, particularly in a short series, but we honestly believed we had the better team and that we would beat them.

When I give my reasons for our not beating the Celtics, it sounds like sour grapes. But I honestly believe we could have beaten them and would have beaten them had it not been for a few key injuries we suffered. Midway through the season, we lost our best big defensive forward, Phil Jackson, and never got him back. Late in the season, we lost one of our best offensive forwards, Cazzie Russell.

Cazzie broke an ankle and missed the last two months. He tried to come back in the Boston playoff series and gave it a great try, but he just couldn't do it. He played in only five games and averaged about 2 points a game. During the season, he had averaged more than 18 points a game.

Playing without Jackson and, you might as well say, without Russell, we just wore out against the Celtics. We were going with six men, and it was just too much for us.

It was amazing that we went as far as we did. There was no question in our minds that with a completely sound ball club we would have beaten them. We still might have if Frazier hadn't gotten hurt in the fifth game.

That was the game in which the momentum seemed to shift in our favor. Boston had beaten us three of the first four, but we won the fifth game to make it three games to two. We figured the Celtics were an old ball club and that we were in a good spot to take the last two games and win the division championship.

But Frazier pulled a groin muscle in that fifth game and, although he tried to play in the sixth game, he just couldn't do the things he wanted to do. As it was, we lost by only 1 point to Boston and we were eliminated.

A lot of people wondered what might have happened if we had had Jackson and Russell for the playoffs or if we at least had had a sound Walt Frazier in that sixth game. We thought we knew what would have happened. We would have gone all the way. There was no question in our minds that, with everything being equal, with a complete ball club, we would have beaten Boston in that series.

One of the ironies of that playoff series is that one of the Celtics who hurt us most was our old teammate, and my old roommate, Emmette Bryant. Emmette played a fantastic series. He was the star of two of their victories and he was in our hair throughout the series.

Ever since I began playing in New York, Emmette and I used to get together during the summer to do a little fishing. Even after he left the Knicks, we always managed to fish together.

After we were eliminated, one of the writers asked me if I was going to go fishing with Emmette that summer.

"Yes," I said, "only this time I'm going to use him for bait."

We were disappointed, of course, but there was no wailing

or gnashing of teeth in our dressing room after that sixth game; there were no tears, no swearing, no feeling sorry for ourselves and no promises made about next year.

We knew we had a ball club that was championship potential right there. I remember sitting around the dressing room after that sixth game, talking to DeBusschere and both of us agreeing that next year would be our year.

We can take it, we said. Let's come into training camp ready.

The same feeling carried right through to training camp the following summer. The transition had been made on the Knickerbocker ball club. The trades had been made to strengthen the team. The club was set. We had looked very good in the second half the previous season, the guys had played together very well and they had confidence in one another and in themselves.

We knew if we played for the entire 1969–70 season the way we had played in the second half of 1968–69, we would be champions. And everybody pushed extra hard to achieve that goal.

Nothing was said; there were no training-camp speeches by Red or any of the players. We all went about our business quietly but efficiently, and with great determination. It was a kind of unspoken thing, a known thing that everybody carried within him and needed not to be said.

These are a couple of the guys we were going to do it with. Dave DeBusschere is in the middle, next to Dick Barnett. *(United Press International Photo)*

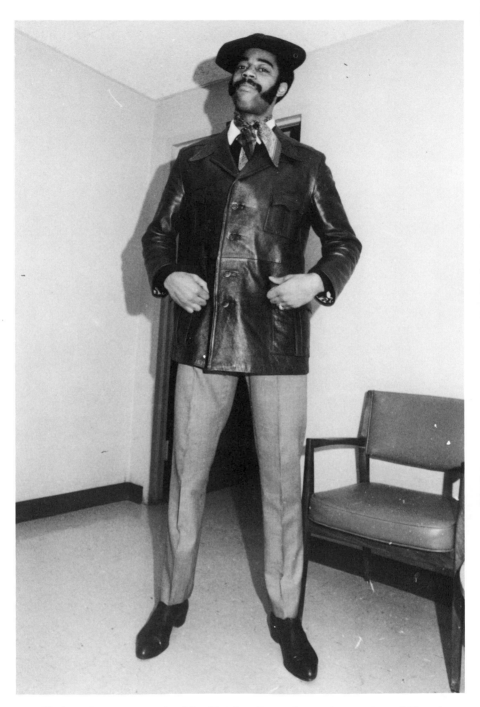

Clyde is the Joe Namath of the Knicks. *(United Press International Photo)*

13
Cast of Characters

It takes years of hard work and experience to make a champion. It takes careful planning and intelligent drafting of college players. It takes a trade here and there to fill in the missing pieces. And it takes someone to instill a feeling of unity and a desire to win once the right players are assembled.

It took the Knicks six years to complete their cast of characters which would bring a professional basketball championship to New York after twenty-four long, hard, frustrating years.

The first piece in the puzzle was Willis Reed. The others soon followed. Bill Bradley, Walt Frazier, Cazzie Russell, Dave Stallworth, Bill Hosket, Don May, Phil Jackson, Mike Riordan and John Warren all came in the draft, with Eddie Donovan and Red Holzman shrewdly selecting from the college crop.

Three others came in trades. Dick Barnett arrived from the Los Angeles Lakers in 1965. Nate Bowman was purchased from the Seattle SuperSonics in 1967. And in 1968 Dave DeBusschere was obtained from the Detroit Pistons to provide the missing piece in the championship puzzle.

163

*Now the cast of characters was set. The NBA champion-
ship was the Knicks' for the taking.*

You don't win a championship with one
superstar and you don't win a championship with five players and you don't win a championship with eight players.
You win a championship with twelve players, each one doing his job.

The New York Knickerbockers' 1969–70 NBA championship belonged to twelve men, the least of them as important
as all the rest.

Some of them are gone now, but they left with something
that nobody can ever take away from them. No matter what
they do, no matter where they go, they will always be able
to say that for one year they played on a team that was the
greatest in professional basketball.

They are champions all!

DAVE DEBUSSCHERE. Dave is one of the leaders on the
team, one of the unsung heroes. He's the kind of guy who
has a job to do and goes out and does it every night. He does
it if he's hurting or if he's tired and he does it without com-
plaining.

Most of all, I respect him as a man. He's a really good guy,
a guy who doesn't hold back his beliefs or his opinions. He'll
come to the defense of anybody if he thinks they're right.
He's going to go along with what he believes is right. And
he's going to go along with what's best for the ball club. All
he wants to do is win.

He has a tough job being a small man playing forward. He
does a fantastic job even though he is usually at a height
disadvantage. For his size—he's a shade under 6–6, but he's
considered our big forward and he's always assigned to
guard the other team's big forward—I think, pound for
pound, he's as rugged as any individual playing the game.

He admits to me that he's the worst shooter on the starting
team, but he's really one of the best long-distance jump

Dave DeBusschere: I respect him as a man. *(United Press International Photo)*

shooters around. He can hit from a long way out, although his primary responsibility is under the boards.

The responsibility for the rebounding lies with Dave and me. We represent the bulk of the rebounding as a team, although Walt Frazier gives us a tremendous amount of help. We're not a big team and not a great rebounding team, so Dave's job is doubly important. And he's probably the best defensive forward in the league.

When he played against us, I always respected Dave as a terrific ballplayer. One thing I remember about him is that he always put out. He always gave of himself; he didn't hold back.

When I first heard about the trade that brought Dave to the Knicks, I liked it. I was glad to know we were getting him. You always hate to see teammates get traded, but when we got DeBusschere, I knew I was going back in the middle and I was happy about that. The only reservation I had about the trade was Dave's ankle. He had had trouble with his ankle and I was worried about it. But if the ankle was all right, I knew we'd be getting a terrific ballplayer.

As it turned out, Dave's ankle was all right and we did get a terrific ballplayer . . . and a terrific man.

WALT FRAZIER. You know Clyde. It's his show. It's his ball; he just lets us play with it once in a while. He's a tremendous ballplayer. I don't think even he knows how good he is.

The man has the quickest hands I've ever seen—the fastest hands in the East, or the West, for that matter. He says he can catch three flies at one time, and I don't doubt him. And I like what Bill Hosket said about him. "Clyde," Hos said, "is the only man who can strip a car while it's going forty miles an hour."

He triggers a lot of the stuff on the defense for us with his fast hands. His steals help make our defense work.

He not only plays what players call "the good *D*" (for defense), he helps Dave and me a lot on the boards. He comes in and gives us a big hand. He's a good rebounder for

When we need points, Dick Barnett comes through. *(George Kalinsky)*

a guard because he has an instinct for the ball, and since we're basically a small team, we need that rebounding help.

Clyde is a very good shooter; he puts out all the time; he plays the game. He knows what he has to do and does it. He knows if our offense is going to go, he's got to be the man to keep it going for us because he controls the ball most of the time. He makes us go. As far as the Knicks are concerned, Clyde is the quarterback. He's the Joe Namath of the Knicks—and in more ways than one.

He's a happy-go-lucky guy. Everything is going his way right now, so there is no need for him to worry about anything. He's a flashy dresser. Danny Whelan gave him the name "Clyde" because of his clothes. He saw the movie *Bonnie and Clyde* and began wearing clothes like Clyde Barrow—big floppy hats and spats and bell-bottoms. Danny called him Clyde and the nickname just stuck with him.

DICK BARNETT. The elder statesman of the ball club, Dick is a guy who always does his job. He has as good a training habit as anybody on the team. He's an ideal player, always in shape and ready to play.

He and I have played together longer than anybody on the team. I remember when he first came to the Knicks. It was my second year with the team and I was playing forward and he was playing guard and he used to get picked more than anybody I ever saw in my life. The forward used to set a pick for him and he used to just lay up there on the guy and I'd have to switch to the guard.

I used to tell him: "Look, man, I'm in enough trouble trying to guard these forwards and you're going to keep calling a switch and make me play these fast little guards. Try to get over these picks, will you?"

We used to laugh over that.

I guess I should explain right here what a pick is. Say Barnett is guarding Oscar Robertson, for example. Oscar's teammate might set a block, or pick, which separates Robertson from his defensive man (Barnett). Dick must either go around the pick or he will call "switch" and another man will have to pick up Robertson to help Barnett out.

Dick works as hard as anybody on the team. People keep talking about his getting old, but management didn't put him up in expansion, so they must not think he's getting old. The man doesn't play like he's getting old. Why does age have to be a criterion? Why can't ability be the criterion?

He goes out and does his job. He does it every night. He's a good basketball player, one of the best shooters in the league. You know he can shoot, there's no question about that. I have confidence in him. I like to see him shoot. I know he's an old pro; he'll give it all he's got. He's not one of those guys who'll be on tonight and off tomorrow. He works at it every night.

Down the stretch, when we need points, Dick comes up with a lot of big baskets for us. He's the kind of ballplayer who says, "It's my job to do it," and he does it.

Dick has a slow way of walking and a strange way of running that make him look like he's loafing. He has been accused many times of loafing. But anybody who has ever played with him doesn't think he loafs. He's a good man. You know he works. He works on the defense and he works on the offense. And he knows the game. A lot of times he can be having a bad night and he won't shoot the ball at all. The ball's not going down for him, so instead of putting it up and maybe hurting the team, he just won't shoot. Instead, he'll try to give it to somebody else.

He has a quick mind, on and off the court. He's a good businessman and an excellent cardplayer and he has a great knowledge of the game of basketball. And he has the respect of his teammates. There have been rumors that Red Holzman is going to quit as coach, and I assume, at his age, that Barnett would be a likely prospect to take over. At least I've heard that is a possibility. I don't know if that's true or not. They don't consult me on such matters. But I'll tell you this, I think Dick would make a great coach. I know I wouldn't mind playing for him.

Off the court, Dick is something of a comedian. When he's out in public, he can be really sophisticated. But when he's with the guys, he's fun to be around. If you're sitting around with him, he'll have you laughing all night long, telling stories about guys' girl friends, guys he's played with, guys he used to play against, things he did when he was growing up in Gary, Indiana, or when he was playing at Tennessee A & I. He keeps the guys loose and everybody enjoys him for that. He's just a lot of fun, a great guy to play with.

BILL BRADLEY. When Cazzie Russell got hurt, that's when Bill developed into a steady ballplayer. Offensively, he's not as good as Cazzie, but all around with the guys we play with as a unit, he fits into the mold a little better. He plays good defense, is completely unselfish and is a great passer. With Bradley on the team we were able to keep Cazzie on the bench to come off when we needed a lift.

Bill loves to play. He's dedicated to the game. Most of the time when we need a shot, he's the one we go to for the open shot, especially when we're going to work it off a pick. He's a consistently accurate shooter and he gets the ball away quickly.

When he first joined the team, he was very quiet. He had a lot of pressure on him from the newspapers and he was trying to fit in, to find his place. We were having our troubles at that time, and a lot of people expected him to solve them and he couldn't—not all alone. It just wasn't a completely ideal situation.

Now Bill is a valuable member of our team. The guys give him a hard time, but he adjusts; he fits in well with the team. Barnett and the rest of the fellows are always teasing him about the way he dresses, but he takes it in stride. Somebody picked an All-NBA worst-dressed team with ten members on it. Bradley made the first team and, believe me, he deserved it. He worked hard for that honor with his white socks and cuffs on his pants and button-down collars.

I always call him Bradley. I call all the players by their last name; it's a habit you get into in sports. One day Bill and I

Bill Bradley: a dedicated player. *(George Kalinsky)*

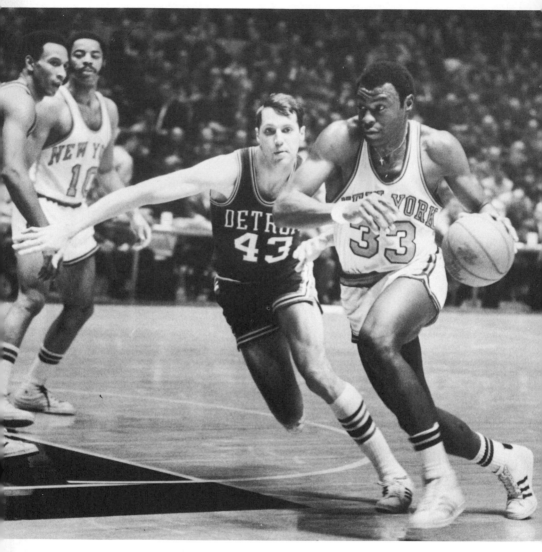

Cazzie Russell gives us a shot in the arm. *(United Press International Photo)*

were standing together in an airport and a fan came up to me and said, "Aren't you Willis Reed?"

I told him I was, and he said, "Can I have your autograph?"

I said sure and I signed my name. Then I turned toward Bradley.

"Don't you know who this is?" I asked the fan. "It's Bradley, Rhodes Scholar, All-American from Princeton University. Don't you want his autograph too?"

Bill just blushed. Later in the day he came over to me and said, "Say, Willis, I want to talk to you."

"Yeah, what's going on, man?"

"Do me a favor," he said.

"Sure, what is it?"

"Don't call me Bradley. Call me Bill."

He doesn't want people to call him Bradley; he wants them to call him Bill. He wants to be one of the boys. But he is one of the boys.

When he had a bad ankle and I saw him with all that tape on his ankle, I climbed all over him.

"Cream-puff ballplayer," I said. "They don't make those guys from Princeton as tough as they used to. All that tape and all. Bud Palmer never wore any tape on his ankle."

When I hurt myself in the playoffs, he came to me just before the seventh game. I was in the whirlpool, and he just looked at me and said: "Cream-puff ballplayer. They don't make those guys from Grambling as tough as they used to."

CAZZIE RUSSELL. He's the original happy-go-lucky kid. He's always talking, talking, talking, about his golf game, about politics, about religion, about anything. You knew there was something wrong if you walked into the dressing room and didn't hear his mouth going. That meant there was trouble.

He did his job though. He could come off the bench and really get us going. He was our ace in the hole. When we needed a lift, Cazzie gave us that shot in the arm. Having him on the bench made us a better team.

I think Cazzie is going to benefit from being traded to the Warriors. He'll get a chance to play more than he did with us and he can be a star in this league. He has that kind of ability. I guess he was pretty close to being the best shooter on our team. He's a streak shooter. A lot of guys can hit two or three in a row, then miss one, then hit two more. Cazzie is the kind who can get the hot hand and hit eight, nine, ten in a row. He can blow a game wide open by himself. That's why he was so valuable coming off the bench. He can just go boom . . . boom . . . boom . . . boom . . . boom . . . and in three minutes he'll have 10 points.

Sometimes he would get down on himself and I'd have to have a talk with him. I told him just to do his job and things would work out. He was important, and I wanted him to know he was important. He got paid for the job he was doing. When you play for a winning team, your value has to be greater, whether you're starting or not.

As captain of the team, I figure it's my job to talk to a player when he gets down. It's important to the team. A player gets peeved at the coach and the coach might never know about it. I feel it's my job to talk to him, to keep harmony on the team. If I see that a player is peeved, I'll talk to him for the good of the team.

The other players made me captain and I take the job seriously. But even if I wasn't captain, I might talk to players when they have problems. It's our job to do that—not one man's job, but everybody's job to keep things running smoothly.

If I don't do my job or Dave doesn't do his or Clyde doesn't do his, we're hurt. It's like Red says, the most important guys on the team are the ones on the bench because they only play so many minutes a night and they have to be ready to play those few minutes a night and not hurt us.

Of course, Cazzie is absolutely fanatic about physical fitness. "Muscles Russell" we call him because he's always doing calisthenics and isometrics and drinking carrot juice and eating wheat germ.

During the playoffs, we all got a big kick out of it when he missed that dunk shot against Milwaukee. We didn't think it was so funny at the time, but later we did—when we won. You know Cazzie had a tough time living that one down. All the guys climbed all over him that night. That's part of being a member of a team. The guys are going to give you a hard time when you goof, and Cazzie showed the kind of stuff he is made of because he didn't let it get him down when he missed the dunk. He came back and made two important foul shots later in the game.

We have this thing where we present a game ball to the player who makes the worst shot of the night. You can bet Cazzie got it that night. In fact, Cazzie got it a lot of nights. He always would say, "No, no, not me. So-and-so took a worse shot than me." But everybody would get on him, and he'd wind up getting the game ball. Believe me, Cazzie is going to be missed around here.

DAVE STALLWORTH. Dave is a tremendous ballplayer. I thought he was really on his way before he came down with heart trouble. He does a lot of things well. He handles the ball unusually well for a big man, he runs well and he can shoot. He's another of those players who can come off the bench and give you a lift.

I remember when DeBusschere had some trouble with his ankle and missed three or four games, Stalls came in and played in his place. We won all of those games even with DeBusschere out, which gave the team a big boost.

Dave's got a great attitude toward this game and a great attitude toward life. He's always in a happy mood. He makes you feel happy just being around him. He does a good psych job on the guys who play against him. They may be giving him a hard time, pushing him around, but he won't say a thing. Then he'll score a basket against them and he'll just smile at them with that big, gold-toothed smile of his.

I couldn't believe it when I heard he had a heart ailment. I figured somebody made a mistake. You just don't figure on a man his age coming up with that kind of ailment. I imagined myself being in the same position. One day you're

We were all happy to see Dave Stallworth come back. *(George Kalinsky)*

playing basketball and the next day the man says it's all over for you. It's not like hurting yourself with a bad injury.

When he came back, I was happy for him, but I really wasn't surprised. All the guys were glad to see him back. I think everybody was just hoping he'd be able to work himself back in and contribute a little. Stalls did more than that. He had a great year. He made a big contribution and he was especially good in the playoffs.

MIKE RIORDAN. Another tremendous ballplayer with an enormous desire to play the game is Mike Riordan. That's what makes him what he is. You know he's going to give you everything he's got whether he's having a good night or an off night.

You know Mike always gives you 100 per cent. He's one of those hard-nosed ballplayers who doesn't hold back a thing. He's won some big games for us. He plays a good strong game on defense, has a good drive and keeps improving his shooting because he works so hard.

Personally, the thing that stands out about Mike is that he eats hot dogs. He eats hot dogs all the time. And he's always reading any paper he can get his hands on. He's too much. He's the typical New Yorker, the only native New Yorker on the team, and the guys are always giving him a hard time. They blame him for everything that's wrong with New York City. He gets flustered sometimes, but he takes it and he'll give it right back to them. He's a good guy.

PHIL JACKSON. Phil missed the entire championship year because he had had a back operation the year before, but he was still part of us. He's a champion too. The toughest thing for him was sitting on the sidelines watching us go all the way. I can imagine how he felt being with us, yet not being able to play.

It's unbelievable how good Phil is defensively. He does a lot of good things for us. He has wide shoulders and long arms, and even though you think you're beating him, he still gets past you. He recovers very well on defense. You think

Mike Riordan is truly a New York Knick. *(United Press International Photo)*

you've outrebounded him, but his long arms are reaching up to get the ball.

In the words of the players on the team, he's a nut. He's the team hippie. He comes on strong with his pipe in his mouth and sounds like an intellectual. He's a really good guy, but a bad cardplayer. I guess that's the reason Barnett is always looking for him.

NATE BOWMAN. He did a good job filling in for me and giving me a blow. He was very important to the ballclub and especially important to me. Without him, there would be nobody to give me a rest. And some nights he did an exceptional job. Nate is a fun guy, a good guy to be with socially. He's always teasing people, especially Danny and Red. Red was always telling him, "Nate, you're my main man." He's a basketball fanatic. He'd drop anything and go anywhere just to see a basketball game.

BILL HOSKET. My old roomie Bill is another really good guy. I think he's going to develop into a good ballplayer in this league if he ever gets the chance. He was going to get that chance in Buffalo and then he tore his Achilles tendon. He can shoot and he can rebound and he knows the game. The only question is his knee. He had it operated on, and it looks like it's going to be all right. Hos is a very sincere person and very dedicated about the game. He wants to play. He wants to do well and he will. Bill is a very intelligent person, a very thoughtful person, and a good friend.

DONNIE MAY. Donnie was very quiet and very strange— a hard guy to get to know. You'd hardly ever know he was around, and he'd be the first one out of the dressing room after a game. He really never got a chance to show what he could do with us. His problem is his height. It's hard to play the forward spot in the NBA when you're only 6–4, and he's not a good enough ball handler to play guard. But he can play. He proved that when he got the chance to play regularly with Buffalo. He became an outstanding player. He's got a good outside shot and he's tough around the basket. The only problem is he can't put the ball down on the floor. Around the basket, though, where he can get the ball off the boards or make one or two dribbles before shooting, he is really tough. And for standing shots, just getting the ball and letting go, he'll make most of them. He's an excellent shooter. I think he will help a team by being a guy who can come off the bench and hurt the opposition shooting, a lot like Cazzie did for us.

JOHN WARREN. My other old roomie, my main man, John is a really good ballplayer. I was sorry to see him go. I think he's going to be an outstanding ballplayer. He's tough and he was the quickest player on our team. He's fast, he can jump and he can shoot the basketball. John plays good defense, handles the ball well and knows the game.

He was like my little brother; I guess I was closer to him and Hosket than to anybody else on the team. There isn't anything in the world I wouldn't do for John. I wish him all the luck in the world. I'm glad he got a chance to play and to show what he could do, but I really miss him.

John was drafted by the Cleveland Cavaliers; May and Hosket were drafted by the Buffalo Braves, who also got Nate Bowman in a trade. That was after the 1969–70 season, and with Phil Jackson returning to the active roster, that left room for three players. The spots were filled by the following, all good additions:

MIKE PRICE. Mike was our first pick from Illinois, so he became my roommate. And he's a good one. He's also a good basketball player. He has the ability to play in this league. He plays good defense, he's got excellent speed and he's strong and a good jumper. All he needs is experience, which he'll get with this ball club. We've become very close. He's much more outgoing than Warren. John was quiet; Mike says what he thinks—right or wrong. He's a good student of the game and a good roommate. He sleeps a lot.

EDDIE MAST. Eddie has a lot of ability; his problem is channeling it the right way. He's not mature yet. He's twenty-two and thinks the whole thing is a big merry-go-round. When I was twenty-two, I was playing for a living, battling guys who were thirty years old for my bread. He recently got married and maybe that will help him mature, get some responsibility and become a better player. He's going to have to get stronger, but he has the moves. He's a nice kid. He tends to be the hippie type, with his long hair. The guys call him "Psychedelic" and tease him about his hair. He takes it good-naturedly and that's good. It's important on a ball club to have guys who can laugh and kid with one another without losing their temper.

GREG FILLMORE. This, very possibly, is the man who will take my job someday. He's very young, has no experience and is very unsure of himself. With work and confidence, he'll get better, and I invited him to my camp during the summer to work with him. He's not a very good shooter, but he can work to become better. With his height and his instincts around the basket, he'll do the job on offense. He joined us in midseason, which was a disadvantage. The first time I saw him, I said, "This guy can't even shoot the ball. He palms it too much." But I noticed that he was surprisingly quick for his size and he was strong. He has good legs, but he needs to get rid of some baby fat. He's really a nice kid. At first, he was so quiet he hardly said a word. But as he got to be more familiar with the guys, I realized he has a sense of humor and is a lot of fun. The guys joke with him a lot. I think he'll be around a long time, and it wouldn't surprise me if Greg is the next center for the Knicks.

Lew Alcindor made the Bucks the team to beat in our division. *(United Press International Photo)*

14
End of a Perfect Year

It was one of those years. One of those unbelievable years in which everything goes right.

It started with news that Bill Russell had retired, never again to work his intimidating magic against NBA rivals, and right there the Boston Celtics' professional basketball dynasty came to a screeching halt.

Then it was October 14, 1969, opening night for the Knicks in Madison Square Garden. They beat the Seattle SuperSonics. Then they won in Chicago and Cincinnati and came home to add Los Angeles and Phoenix to the list of wins.

San Francisco ended the streak at five, but then it started all over. Detroit. Baltimore. Atlanta. San Diego. Milwaukee. Phoenix. San Diego again. The streak went to sixteen, and people began to get excited; people began to realize that this was a special year.

Atlanta fell on November 26 under a devastating display of Knick power. The score was 138–108; the victory streak was a record-tying seventeen in a row.

Two nights later it was Cincinnati in Cleveland, and this was the most amazing game of all. Down by 5 points with

183

sixteen seconds left to play, the Knicks came back to win the game and break the all-time NBA winning streak. Nothing could stop them now.

You could tell, right from training camp, that this year was going to be something special. You couldn't tell it from what was said, but rather from the way the fellows worked.

We didn't talk about it, but we knew we had a team that was good enough to go all the way. And we all worked with that objective in mind. There was an air of confidence and determination in camp.

I can remember two high spots during the season that gave us the idea we could do just about anything. The first was when we scored 6 points in the last sixteen seconds to beat Cincinnati and break the NBA record for consecutive victories. It was our eighteenth and it was just an unbelievable finish. You would have to say it is practically impossible to score 6 points in sixteen seconds, especially with the twenty-four second clock, but we did it. It also gave us a record of 23–1 for our first twenty-four games.

The second high spot I remember was Christmas night in Madison Square Garden. Before a packed house, we beat Detroit with one second to go with one of our out-of-bounds plays.

We got off to such a great start and opened such a big lead over the rest of the teams in our division that it looked like we were just going to run away with it. Of course, it's almost impossible for a team, any team, to go through an entire season without at least one little slump.

Our slump came in January. All of a sudden all of the things we were doing right we stopped doing. I can't explain why a team goes into a slump any more than I can explain why a player goes into a slump. I guess it has a lot to do with momentum and confidence.

When you're winning, you build up that momentum and you have the feeling that you can go out on the court and beat anybody you play. So much of sports is confidence. When you lose a couple, you begin to have doubts—doubts about your own ability. So maybe you do things a little more cautiously, a little more thoughtfully, and the more cautious you are the tighter you become. You can't play basketball— or any sport, for that matter—when you're tight. The next thing you know you've lost that confidence and you're in a slump where you just can't do anything right.

Maybe we were just getting tired from all the traveling and playing three or four games a week. I know I was tired. I was also having a little trouble with my stomach and I just wasn't doing things the way I had done them earlier in the year.

I admit I was a little concerned about the slump—mine and the team's. Usually, there are two cures for a slump. You can rest or you can just go out and work a little harder and hope that things straighten themselves out.

I knew I couldn't afford to rest. I had to continue on the grind, and it does get to be a grind with all the traveling and all the demands on your time for appearances and interviews. We were getting a lot of attention in the press, and, as captain and center, I was getting more than my share. The more I got, the more demands there were. You go into a town and you're asked to go on this radio show or that television show. Or there are requests for newspaper or magazine interviews. You try to be selective, but you can't turn them all down, and it takes up a lot of your time.

It's worse in New York, where there are more radio and television shows, more newspapers and magazines. It's hard to say no to people in your own town.

Another problem is friends who call me at the hotel. They mean well, and I try to be nice and friendly to them. But just figure that if six people call (and that's a conservative estimate) and I spend ten minutes on the telephone talking with each of them, that's an hour gone out of my day—an hour that I could have been resting or practicing or just concentrating on the job ahead of me.

Sometimes you can overextend yourself to the point

We got over the Bucks, and only the Lakers stood in our path. *(Malcolm W. Emmons)*

where you are neglecting your primary job—basketball. Since there would be no rest for me, I just had to go and work a little harder to get myself straightened out.

I have my own personal thing to try to pull myself out of a slump. It's a funny thing about being an athlete. Sometimes you can get down when you're not playing well or the team is not playing well, and you have to go back and pick up your scrapbook and read about some of the things that you have done in the past. You have to go back and rebuild that confidence in yourself, really psych yourself up.

I started keeping a scrapbook in high school, but when I got with the Knicks, I just didn't have time to keep one. People kept them for me. Friends or fans kept them and sent them to me, and I like to look back over them when I'm feeling down. I especially like to look at my high school scrapbook. There's an item in there that I get a kick out of seeing. It's from a Bernice paper about when we went to the state championships. The headline said:

REED COLLECTS 45;
WESTSIDE GOES TO STATE

That was one of the biggest moments in my life.

Sometimes you just have to look back and see how things have been. I've done that on numerous occasions. I did that when we had our little slump in January of our championship year. After you read some of your clippings, you feel like you can go out there and fight the world.

During our little slump, the Milwaukee Bucks got hot and made a serious run at us. A lot of people thought they were going to overtake us, but fortunately our slump didn't last too long. We straightened out and finished ahead of Milwaukee by five games.

It was the first time in sixteen years the Knicks had finished first in their division, but it didn't set off any wild celebration. We clinched it in San Diego by beating the Rockets and right after the game we had to catch a plane to Los Angeles. Frank Blauschild, Director of Public Relations and now Assistant General Manager, sent out for pizzas, and we celebrated our success by eating pizza in the San Diego airport at one in the morning.

We all knew there really wasn't anything to celebrate. We hadn't done anything yet. Our job wouldn't be finished until we won it all—the NBA championship.

We still had a long road ahead. First we had to play the Baltimore Bullets and if we got by them, either the Philadelphia 76ers or the Milwaukee Bucks. We figured it would be the Bucks and we figured they would be tough from the way they improved in the second half of the season.

First, though, we had the Bullets. They're a tough team with a lot of great individual players and a good bench, and we knew they were going to have the proper motivation. They were dying to get revenge for the previous year when we knocked them off four straight in the playoffs after they had finished first in the division.

We won the first two games and we were coming home for the third game. The writers began saying that we were a cinch, that we probably would sweep them four straight again, that we had the Indian sign on them. I must admit I felt pretty good about our chances, but we didn't think we were a cinch. You still have to go out there and do it. The other team was not going to lay down for us. Professional athletes don't lay down; they keep fighting until they are eliminated.

Wes Unseld played a fantastic game in that third game, and I played a terrible one. He grabbed 34 rebounds; I had 5. He scored 23 points; I had 12. That was the difference and I knew it. We had let the Bullets off the hook. They beat us in our own arena, and it had to give them a tremendous lift.

They won the fourth game in Baltimore and tied the series, two games each. Now I knew they were going to be tough. Again Unseld outplayed me, and I was feeling a little dejected and a lot determined.

Now we came down to a game we had to win. If we lost, we'd have to go back to Baltimore in a "must" situation and we knew the Bullets would be especially tough on their home court if they needed that one victory to eliminate us.

That fifth game was a game we needed and we played to our fullest potential. We beat them by 21, holding them to 80 points, in a game that almost reached perfection, especially our defense.

Personally, it was a very satisfying victory. After two bad games, I had my best game of the series—36 points, 36 rebounds. One more win and we'd have the Bullets out of our hair.

Back in Baltimore, we let them off the hook again and the series came down to the seventh game. It was the biggest game of the year for us, bigger than the fifth game in one important respect. If we lost, we'd be eliminated; there would be no way to come back.

I remember sitting in front of my locker in our dressing room before that seventh game and thinking:

What are you going to do if you lose this game? You're going to go to Louisiana and try to go fishing and you're going to sit there with your line in the water and think about losing this game. You're going to have to drive through Baltimore on your way to Louisiana and you're going to have to think that these people beat you in the playoff even though, in your heart, you knew you were a better ball club.

It was like a nightmare. I knew we simply had to win this game. A lot of the guys had looked into the mirror and said to themselves: "Let's see what kind of man you are tonight. If you're a ballplayer, stand up and prove it."

I knew we were going to play that night. I knew we were going to get that effort. There was never any question about our having a bad game. These are the kind of guys we have on our team, guys who can, when the game means the most, play at their best. And this game meant a lot. This was a game they could really get up for and be ready to play.

And we were ready. We really came up for that seventh game. As usual we played our best in a crucial situation. Again, we felt there was no cause for a celebration. Now we had to get by the Milwaukee Bucks.

We beat the Bucks in five games, but that is no indication of how tough they were. We just played outstanding basket-

First Unseld, then Alcindor and now Wilt. *(Darryl Norenberg)*

ball. We got a lift twice from Cazzie Russell, who came off the bench to fire us to two victories.

Lew Alcindor played a sensational series. He was almost impossible to stop. Fortunately, for us, basketball is a five-man game, not a one-man game, and we beat the Bucks and moved into the championship finals against the Los Angeles Lakers.

The Lakers presented new problems with their three superstars, Wilt Chamberlain, Elgin Baylor and Jerry West. When we lost one of the first two games at home, it made our job that much tougher. Now we had to win one out of two games in Los Angeles just to stay even.

We won the third game, but I'll never know how. We were just awful in the first half, but we came back and went ahead, and it looked like we had the game won when DeBusschere sank a jumper with three seconds left. The Lakers took the ball out; Jerry West had it and I was back there with him, but I wasn't contesting him too closely because I didn't want to foul him.

I didn't think Jerry would shoot from that distance. And when he shot, I never expected it to go in. It went clean through without touching anything but the net. They said it was a 55-foot shot. I could hardly believe my eyes.

That's the kind of thing that takes the heart out of a team, but the Knicks have plenty of heart to spare. We beat them in overtime and when we lost the fourth game, also in overtime, we still came home tied at two games apiece. It was a good position to be in because two of the last three games were going to be played in the Garden.

Then came the fifth game in Madison Square Garden, the game I'll never forget if I live to be a hundred. All of a sudden, it looked like our perfect year had come to an end.

I knew I was hurt when I went down. *(United Press International Photo)*

15

"We're Going to Win It for You"

Including exhibitions and playoffs, the New York Knickerbockers were playing in their 109th game of the season. And that 109th game—the fifth game of the National Basketball Association championship playoffs— was just eight minutes old when it happened, the thing the Knicks had feared since they started their drive to a championship some eight months before in training camp.

Willis Reed, captain and center, heart and soul, strength and inspiration of the Knicks, was hurt. Driving to the basket, he suddenly crumpled to the floor as if he had been shot. He looked like a beached whale as he lay there in a helpless heap, writhing in agony, his face contorted in pain. Willis Reed was hurt. Willis Reed was hurt badly.

There were 19,500 people in Madison Square Garden that night, 19,500 voices raised to a pitch in anticipation of what they were certain would follow. Now, 19,500 voices let out a gasp in unison. Now, 19,500 voices were stilled, and the silence was eerie.

There was fear in the air and concern on the faces of Willis Reed's teammates. The scoreboard showed the Lakers

193

*held a 10-point lead, and the pain on his face showed that
Willis Reed was going to play no more basketball that night
—maybe no more basketball that season. If that was true, if
Willis Reed was hurt that badly, then there would be no way
for the Knicks to win their first championship in their
twenty-four-year history. No way.*

When I went down, I knew I was hurt
bad. I could feel the pain in my right hip, like somebody was
sticking a knife in there and then twisting the knife after
plunging it in. My first thought was that this was the end of
a beautiful season . . . and what a way for it to end!

I've heard it said that people, when they are dying, can
see their whole life pass before them. In a way, that's what
I experienced as I lay there on the Madison Square Garden
floor trying to hide my pain from 19,500 people.

I thought of all the work that had gone into getting me this
far. Here we were, just two games away from being world
champions, which is what we had all worked so hard for. I
thought not only of the work I had done that season, beginning with training camp in mid-September, but what I had
gone through since I decided, all the way back in 1956, that
basketball was the game for me.

I thought of all the hard work, the hours of practice, the
thousands of jump shots I had taken, all of it designed with
one end in mind—to play on a world championship team.
And now that I was so close to realizing that goal, this had
to happen. I couldn't help wondering why. Why me? Why
now?

One other thing ran through my mind. I remembered
something I had said to Walt Frazier back in training camp.
Clyde had been hurt during the playoffs the previous two
seasons, and a lot of people believed that if Clyde hadn't
been hurt we would have won a championship. So when
training camp started, I went to Clyde and said, "Look here,
man, we've got a chance to win it all this year, so don't go
getting yourself hurt again."

Trainer Danny Whelan came out; I stayed in the game—but not for long.
(United Press International Photo)

We had a good laugh about that, and now I was the guy who went and got hurt.

I can't remember how it happened. All I know is that I went to make a move on Wilt Chamberlain and as I drove for the basket, I felt a terrible, sharp pain in my hip and down I went.

At first I thought I was seriously hurt and then I thought maybe I wasn't hurt so badly after all. Our trainer, Danny Whelan, came over; I got up and found I could walk. I figured it was just a little pull and it would be all right. I stayed in the game, but I couldn't move at all and the pain was almost unbearable. That's when I knew that I was hurt badly.

Danny helped me to the dressing room during the half, I was finished for the night. I just hoped I wasn't finished for the year. I was very discouraged. To have come this far and have this happen just didn't seem fair. I kept wondering what I had done to deserve this. Maybe it was just not to be for us to win the championship.

I got to thinking about Jerry West and Elgin Baylor, who had never won a championship. I guess it's just not to be for them to play on a championship team. I hope not. I think it's a shame that they haven't been on a championship team with all they've meant to the game and the league. They've been in the finals ten times and never won it. That's got to be tough to take. It must be disheartening. I think it's a shame they've never won, but I wasn't about to give up our championship for them to have a crack at it.

Dr. James Parkes examined me and said I had contusions and a strain of the right tensor muscle, the muscle that runs from the hip to the knee. He gave me a shot of Novocain and a shot of cortisone in the hope that I'd be able to play the second half. But it was no use.

When the guys went out for the second half, Cazzie Russell came over to me. I guess he must have seen the disappointment in my eyes because he said, "Don't worry, big fella, we're going to win it for you."

I was in the dressing room for the entire second half.

There is an intercom from the scorer's table to each dressing room, and I was getting a special play-by-play broadcast from John Condon, the public-address announcer. What I heard sounded like fantasy.

The guys just refused to quit. They kept coming at the Lakers, cutting into their lead and forcing them into costly mistakes. The Lakers kept turning the ball over, and our guys kept converting the turnovers into baskets. I could hear the crowd going wild. They all did a terrific job, DeBusschere, Bradley, Frazier, Stalls, Cazzie, all of them. They were down by 16 at one point, but somehow they came back and won that game. They picked me up. They won without me. Now I was hoping I could get well enough to help pick them up, to help them win one of the next two games.

We flew out to Los Angeles to play the sixth game two days later. I was kind of optimistic. I was hoping I could play that game, that the injury wasn't as bad as most people thought it was, that it would clear up right away and I'd be able to play.

I got out to Los Angeles and went through my treatment —whirlpool, sauna, hot and cold baths. But the injury didn't respond, and Dr. Parkes said I wouldn't be able to play. I could hardly walk. I couldn't lift the leg up. I would be no help to my team, and it was frustrating to just sit there and watch Chamberlain do what he did.

I had the consolation of knowing that at least there was one more game left. Dr. Parkes, Danny Whelan and I took a plane back to New York right after the game while the rest of the team came back the following day. I had a date with Danny at nine o'clock the next morning to continue my treatment. I knew the injury would clear up in due time, but time was something I didn't have. I had less than thirty-six hours.

The pain was so great I could barely jump. *(United Press International Photo)*

16

Number One

Dressed in street clothes, Willis Reed sat on the Knick bench, helpless, watching Wilt Chamberlain demolish the four men who took turns trying to replace the New York center. The frustration built as Wilt scored 45 points, grabbed 27 rebounds and led the Lakers to a one-sided 135–113 victory in the sixth game.

Now it all came down to one last game in New York's Madison Square Garden on Friday night, May 8, 1970. All the months of hard work and preparation, of sweat and pain, of disappointments and heartaches and joys, came down to one game—one game that meant the championship of the National Basketball Association.

And the big question on everyone's mind was: Would Willis Reed play?

Reed had made his decision. He made it sitting on the Knick bench in Los Angeles watching Chamberlain work his personal destruction.

"I'll play," Reed said. "I'll play if I can crawl."

There was never any doubt in my mind that I was going to try to play that seventh game; the doubt in my mind was whether or not I was going to be able to do it.

I don't know what the atmosphere was like in the dressing room before the game because I wasn't there. I was in the trainer's room, which is outside the main part of the dressing room, being worked on by Danny Whelan and Dr. Parkes. One by one my teammates came into the trainer's room and peeked in with a question-mark look on their face. They said hardly anything. I mean what could you say? The look on their faces seemed to say, "Man, I wish it was me instead of you."

Some of them asked me, "Are you going to play; are you going to try?"

I said I would try. I had spent most of the early part of the day in the office of Dr. Parkes, who was the unsung hero of our championship. He got me to play, using part therapy and part psychology.

Then I went over to the Garden where Coach Red Holzman was waiting for me and got into my uniform. It was six o'clock, about an hour and a half before game time. I walked out onto the court and took a few shots, then tried to make a few moves.

"It's still sore," I told Red, "but I can do it."

Red nodded. "Okay," he said. "You're starting."

By the time I got back to the dressing room, the rest of the team was beginning to arrive. I went right to the trainer's room to get worked on again by Dr. Parkes.

I guess I'm an optimist because I thought I would be in better shape to play than I was. As it turned out, I was lucky to play at all and I owe that to Dr. Parkes. He gave me a shot of Carbocaine, which is basically the same as Novocain except that it's much longer lasting. Actually, it was Carbocaine mixed with cortisone and it was injected directly into the hip. The muscle pull was spread over a large area, so the shot didn't do the job I thought it would. There was still a great deal of pain.

But it got the job done enough for me to go out on that court and that was all I was asking for. With a muscle, you can't tell how deep the pull is. It's not like an ankle injury. You can always tell where the injury is in an ankle.

There was never any worry in my mind that I would suffer any permanent injury from playing all shot up. Red had said he wouldn't permit me to play if there was any chance of permanent injury. I thought these were very competent people looking after me, and Dr. Parkes guaranteed me there wasn't going to be any permanent injury. He said rest would make it as good as new and I had a whole summer to rest. But first I had to get through forty-eight minutes of basketball.

Both teams were already on the court taking their pre-game warm-up when I got out there. They had been out there quite some time, and much has been made of my late arrival, which seemed to have a dramatic effect on people. Was it planned? Did Red delay my appearance in an effort to gain a psychological edge? Did he try to decoy the Lakers into thinking I was not coming out and then spring me for a shock effect?

To all those questions, the answer is no. I know it doesn't make as good a story, but this happens to be the truth. Dr. Parkes wanted to wait until the last possible minute to give me the shot because he was only going to shoot me once and he wanted it to last as long as possible once he gave it to me.

Also, it took longer to give me the needle than Dr. Parkes figured. I don't know why. I'm not a doctor, although it seemed like those last few days were the equivalent of one year in medical school. So, my late arrival was completely accidental. It just happened to work to our advantage.

I'd hate to have to go through that again. But I must admit it was worth it. Of all the things a man does in his life, he must have self-contentment. If we had lost that game, or if I hadn't at least tried to play, I would not be self-content. I knew I wouldn't, even though I couldn't have blamed myself for getting hurt when I did.

I knew we had the better ball club man for man. All the pressure put on us all year, everybody saying we were this and we were that, Joe Lapchick saying we were the most exciting team he had ever seen, all these things being said about us—it would have been hard to take to come down to that last game and blow it all, blow the whole season.

I figured, Let's do it now. Let's not think that if we don't win it now, it's because of an injury, and if we don't win it this year, we'll win it next year. You never know what's going to happen next year. We could get a key injury early in the season and that could be the end of the season.

It was evident from the way we played all year that the guys weren't thinking of next year. You never saw these guys loaf, not even with a 20-point lead. The men on this team are proven winners; they go all the way, not half way. They're not guys who are great when the chips are with them; they're just as great when the chips are against them. In fact, they're better when the chips are against them. They played their best under pressure. They proved that in the fifth and seventh games against the Bullets and in the fifth game against the Lakers. Now they were out to prove it again in the seventh game.

In a way, though, it is a shame that you play 110 games and then it all comes down to one game and either you're as great as everybody has been saying you are or you're not— all in one game. After all you've proved in the first 110 games, you still have to go out in that 111th game and prove you deserve what they've been saying about you.

When I stepped out on the court, I got a tremendous ovation from the fans. I know I got a tremendous ovation because I've read so much about it and heard so much about it that it must be true. Frankly, I was not aware of the fans. I had too many other things on my mind. I was in pain for one thing. For another, I knew I had to go out and play a man so many inches taller than me and so much stronger than me, a man who had just had a 45-point game. And I knew I had to go out and play him on one leg. I couldn't run and I really couldn't jump and somehow I was going to have to compensate for all that.

I had enough problems as it was not to be thinking about the fans. If there was going to be any glory for me, it was not

Clyde did it all in the seventh game. *(United Press International Photo)*

going to be when I walked out on the court or even *that* I walked out on the court. If there was going to be any glory, it was going to be after I walked off the court when the forty-eight minutes of basketball were over. All the nice words and all the applause and all the feelings of the fans and all the words in the newspapers that I had a lot of courage to do what I did would not be any consolation to me if we lost.

I'm not putting the fans down. I think they were important to us all year, but even if there was nobody there, the guys were going to play that night. That's the caliber of men we have. If a man's a winner, he's a winner always, not only when he has 19,000 fans cheering for him. I don't care if he's sitting on top of the world or he's down on both hands and knees trying to get up. If he's down on his hands and knees, he's going to try to get up and he's going to get up sooner or later. And if he's on top of the world, he's going to try to stay there.

That's the kind of men we have on the Knicks. They are men you can respect. They have a job to do and they do their job. They work as a unit. That's the reason I think we are successful. We had weaknesses on our ball club, but they were weaknesses we could overcome because we were an intelligent team, and our weaknesses didn't show up.

I think the fans were important to us; fans can inspire you, but if you're not that kind of a man, they can't do a thing for you. We were out there because of Bill Bradley and Dave DeBusschere and Walt Frazier and Dick Barnett and right on down the line. This was the moment of truth in their lives. This was the point where they always dreamed of being, and they were going to go out and prove they deserved to be there.

Some people said that when I came out, it had a great psychological effect on both the Knicks and the Lakers. They said you could tell that the Lakers were visibly disappointed and that they might have lost the game right there.

I find that hard to believe. I think they had to expect me to play. I know Jerry West was quoted as saying he didn't

On the bench in those final minutes, I could hardly wait for it to happen.
(United Press International Photo)

want to win the championship with me sitting on the bench. "Nobody wants to come in the back door," he said. "If he doesn't play, it would take an edge off the championship if we win it."

As far as the players and the press saying we won because I was the inspiration in helping us win, well, that's not for me to say. But if that's what they believe, then I'm grateful. If I helped my team in some small way, that's what I'm supposed to do. That's what I get paid to do.

I knew it was going to be tough trying to guard Wilt on one leg, but I was determined to do the best I could, to use my body against him whenever I could. And it worked. And it was a great feeling when I made the team's first two baskets.

You could sense that the guys were going to play that night. You could feel the excitement in the crowd, and when we took an early lead, it gave us a big lift. I knew we were going to win. I could hardly feel the pain in my hip because I was all charged up.

I had no way of knowing, at the time, that those two baskets would be the only points I would score all night. Later on, somebody asked me how I was going to explain to my son that in the greatest game I ever played, I scored only 4 points and grabbed only 3 rebounds. I don't agree that it was the greatest game I ever played, but it was the most important.

It's funny, I scored 4 points in the first game I ever played in high school and 4 points in the most important game I played as a pro.

All the guys were tremendous that night, especially Frazier. He was fantastic. He scored 36 points and had 19 assists and 7 rebounds.

I played only twenty-seven minutes because we just ran away from them. I was the one who got the shot, but it was as if we were all charged up. By half time we were leading, 69–42. All we had to do was hold them and we'd be champions.

I was on the bench toward the end and I couldn't wait

It was worth the wait. *(United Press International Photo)*

until those final seconds ticked off. And when DeBusschere hugged that ball and the buzzer sounded, we went wild. The whole Garden went wild.

It was a great feeling when I walked off the court. It was a great feeling because we won. I guess I couldn't really enjoy it as much as I would have liked because I was in such pain, but it made life a whole lot easier. And it made the summer a whole lot more enjoyable.

That's the greatest thrill I ever had in basketball. I guess that will always be my big thrill no matter how many years I play, no matter how many championships we win. I can't imagine anything ever topping that.

Whatever else followed, there would never be another time when we would win our first championship, and that made this one something special.

As I walked off the court, not feeling the pain, not feeling anything but happiness, I kept thinking about how it all had started. I thought of all that had gone into this night. I thought all the way back to that clumsy kid in high school and to how much had gone into developing the skills that gave me this chance. And I kept thinking that walking off that court in Madison Square Garden as champions of the world made all the years of practice and all the years of hard work worthwhile.